THE LEISURELY
Hiker's Guide
to Hong Kong
PETE SPURRIER

FormAsia

Contents

MONASTIC HIKES

MUSEUMS HIKES

RESERVOIRS HIKES

SPIRITUAL HIKES

As a foreigner living in Hong Kong, it is easy to exist inside a kind of bubble: travelling between home and office, eating and drinking in the same parts of town, maybe taking the occasional boat out to the islands at weekends but saving longer holidays for trips further afield.

This guide aims to show you that by taking a few steps away from your everyday routine, you can discover nearby attractions you never knew existed – thereby achieving a greater understanding of the city and its culture, and immeasurably enriching your Hong Kong experience.

Following these easy routes will reveal a diversity of discoveries: halls built in honour of a Sung-dynasty princess, and tiny temples overlooking Happy Valley; Hong Kong's only ancient pagoda, and striking views of the Tsing Ma bridge; gun emplacements over the harbour, and organic gardens beside the sea; crystal-clear waterfalls, a hidden cathedral, relics of naval history and fortified villages.

Every one of the hikes in this book ends within striking distance of a cold beer and a plate of chilli prawns. In fact, that's the point: each of these walks can be dashed off in a morning or an afternoon, leaving you plenty of time to enjoy lunch or dinner at a new destination.

It's too often said that Hong Kong cares only for its future and not for its past. We see a welcome change. Recent events involving Wedding Card Street, Wanchai Market, Kom Tong Hall and the Star Ferry have shown that Hong Kong people do care about their shared history, and there is a new will to both preserve the city's built heritage and make it relevant for modern uses.

We've had a fine time researching and photographing this guide, and we've learnt a thing or two on the way. We hope you will enjoy it just as much – and that you will let us know what you find on your own explorations to help us enrich the next edition of the guide with more hiking gems.

Bamboo lush and thick in a secluded valley

Po Lin Monastery

2 HOURS

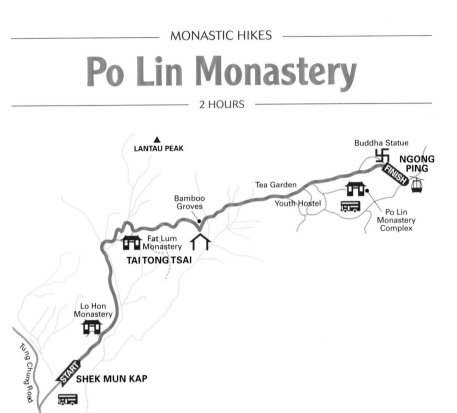

Western Lantau is a spiritual retreat, home to dozens of monasteries, all serenely peaceful except for Po Lin at weekends. Follow in the footsteps of ancient pilgrims by ascending an old trail to reach these holy sites.

Take the MTR to Tung Chung and walk through the bus station to find minibus 34, operated by the New Lantao Bus Company. This little vehicle traverses a meandering route amidst towering new housing estates which occupy what was, until recently, an intensively farmed rural valley. Some buses make a short detour to the old village pier, which is the terminus of the circuitous Tung Chung Road, built by the British Army in the 1960s to connect this remote settlement to the rest of Lantau. Further on, the bus passes a cluster of untidy village houses which conceal the old Tung Chung Fort. This stronghold was built around 1815 by the Viceroy of Guangdong in an attempt to suppress the opium trade.

Last pit-stop before preparing for the climb

Stay on board until the bus terminates at Shek Mun Kap village. Alternatively you can take a blue Lantau taxi to the same point for about $20.

The village shop, next to the bus stop, is your starting point. It's also your last chance to buy water. However, depending on your age and gender, the elderly proprietor may enthusiastically recommend a beer instead.

Look for the track branching uphill to the left. The yellow roof of the Lo Hon Monastery can be seen on the hillside above, and it's not long until you reach the entrance to its grounds. The motorable track ends here. Follow the trail indicated by the blue 'Buddha' character marked on the wall.

For the next half hour or so, the path winds uphill beside an audible stream. It's steep in places but there are pools of clear water to cool your feet. Looking back, you can watch planes taking off from the airport's flat island, and see Tung Chung new town creeping ever closer to this lush valley.

Try to imagine the scene in 1809, when a major naval battle took place in the bay below. Portuguese vessels from Macau helped great Chinese war junks destroy the fleet of the notorious local pirate Cheung Po Tsai, who had been terrorizing the area.

Blue for Buddha, the colour of compassion

A rock pool of crystal clear water from the upper slopes of Lantau Peak

A fork appears; turn right here to cross the stream. Then, before you reach a further bridge, turn up and left to join a much older path of aged stone. This marks the entrance to the Tei Tong Tsai area – a collection of quiet monasteries and pagodas dating back many years, hidden amongst some of Hong Kong's longest-standing bamboo groves. The path between the compounds is easily followed, and leads you over another stone bridge.

Sticks and stones

Mossy trail besides ancient monasteries

Chanting monks are heard but not seen

Take a detour off to the right to see an unusual six-sided pagoda. And keep your ears attuned: if you are lucky, you may hear the methodical drumbeats and resonant tones of Buddhist recitals emanating from a tower hidden among the trees.

Further on, a larger religious compound is found. A bucolic square shaded by trees is a fine place to stop for a breather. All around, Buddhist nuns in grey cloaks and wide-brimmed hats tend vegetable patches and carry water. Turn left here and carry on uphill amidst the scent of wild mint.

The Tei Tong Tsai Buddhist retreat

Now you are mounting the northern flank of Lantau Peak. A rest pavilion is followed by a traditional ornamental gateway — and suddenly the Big Buddha is seen from a distance, its hazy form presiding over as-yet unseen places. Your way lies directly ahead.

A nun's story

After you pass the SG Davis Youth Hostel on your right, you may notice tea plants growing by the path on your left. The high humidity up here allows them to thrive. The tea garden cafés are still in operation, although they no longer seem to offer horse riding – you can find the overgrown corral nearby.

Flourishing tea plantation

Po Lin, now accessible by cable car, offers a colourful spectacle

The track leads you straight into the grounds of the Po Lin Monastery complex, which will be either packed with tourists or completely empty, depending on the day of your visit. Finish off your visit with snacks at the vegetarian canteen.

Founded by three monks in 1905, the 'Precious Lotus' monastery occupied an isolated setting ideally suited for meditative retreat. It remained largely undisturbed until 1993, when 10,000 spectators showed up for the inauguration of the now-famous Big Buddha. The bronze statue represents a bond between old and new: it was constructed in Nanjing by China Aeronautics, a company involved in China's space programme.

Big Buddha watches over Po Lin

Playtime in the Tung Chung fountain

Although cast in sections, it proved too heavy for any helicopter to carry to the lofty site. The alternative meant closing off, for three nights, all roads leading to the monastery – to allow the dismantling of all lamp posts, telegraph poles and electric pylons that might obstruct the oversized trucks transporting such exceptional cargo.

Meditate on this collaboration between ancient wisdom and modern technology as you take your bus back downhill to Tung Chung or Silvermine Bay.

This hike can be made much easier by taking any bus – or, of course, the new Skyrail cable car – up to Po Lin and walking the route in reverse.

Ceramic tradesmen do business

Tradesmen's Temple

1 HOUR

Step to it! The Lo Bun (Master Tradesman) Temple is a unique piece of architecture, and it's located amongst quiet ladder streets and terraces. Follow this route to discover old stairways and back streets of Kennedy Town.

Take any of the high frequency buses 5B, 10 or 104, with convenient stops at the Landmark in Des Voeux Road Central, to their Kennedy Town terminus, and alight at the station. Walk back in the direction whence you came. Here in a small garden stands the foundation stone and arch of the Tung Wah Smallpox Hospital, built in 1901 and demolished after the Second World War. Also conveniently located among the trees is a public toilet.

In 1910 the Smallpox Hospital stood on this location

Take the steps up to Victoria Road, where a wide-crowned banyan stands beside the Bayanihan Centre for foreign domestic helpers. This part of Kennedy Town has changed in character since the tumbledown squatter villages of Mount Davis were removed. Turn left and follow the road until it meets Cadogan Street, and then walk to the waterfront at Kennedy Town New Praya. 'Praya' is a Portuguese word which was imported into the English language by way of Macau, and is used to name several waterfronts in Hong Kong.

The abattoir here is no longer in use, and its triangular pier is now a popular perch for anglers. Follow the praya past the fire station and turn right into Sands Street. A wide flight of steps can be seen ahead. Cross the tram line, take a deep breath and start climbing.

This part of Kennedy Town is much quieter, because the streets are stepped and there is no traffic. Take the first left turn up to Tai Pak Terrace, a charming lane of trees and well-kept potted plants which harks back to a bygone age. The Hong Kong Society for the Promotion of Virtue, an organization encouraging the pursuit of ethics drawn from Buddhism and Taoism, has its home in a graceful old building here.

At the far end, take the steps onto Li Po Lung Path, and continue your journey uphill. A large sign on the retaining wall at the head of the street indicates the way to the temple. Follow it, and you are delivered onto Ching Lin Terrace, another leafy open space, worlds away from the din below.

Escaping the thunder of Belcher's Street

The Tradesmen's Temple is quite a sight with its unique roof design and intricate figurines. Built in 1884, it is dedicated to Si Fu, a master carpenter of ancient times who is viewed as the

Tools of the tradesmen: 19th century bevel-gear drill

patron saint of the construction trade. It was built with funds collected from carpenters, bricklayers and related tradesmen. Beside it, a two-storey structure houses part of Hon Wah Middle School, established in 1949.

Walk to the other end of the terrace. At the steps leading back down, the ornate old street sign is just legible behind years of lichen. Continue up Sands Street and take the next set of steps up to the left, which brings you to To Li Terrace. Here you can enjoy a closer view of the Si Fu Temple's roof sculptures, and of a roof garden on top of the schoolhouse.

The narrower flight of steps at the other end leads up to a spiral staircase, which places you on Pokfulam Road. Turn left past Ricci Hall to find the bus stop: most buses from here pass through Central. Alternatively you can walk down through the Westwood shopping centre to return to Kennedy Town.

Carpenter's inkpot for describing long straight lines

Grooving plane of pine and brass

Mallets of oak for assembly work in cabinet making

Chisels for dovetail and mortise joints

The interior is like the inner-sanctum of a secret society

Unique roof style: Lo Bun temple

Weekend sailors congregate on the beach

BEACHES HIKES

Hobie Cats

2 HOURS

The waters off the southeast of Hong Kong Island – around Tai Tam Harbour and the islands of Po Toi – are some of the SAR's finest for sailing. The calm coasts are popular with those who sail and race by catamaran, particularly the 'hobie' type. One beach has become the centre of action for this sport.

Take the MTR to Shau Kei Wan, exit to the bus station and board bus no. 9, destination Shek O. Ask the driver for 'To Dei Wan' or look out for the Shek O Road bus stop with the Hong Kong Trail mapboard. It's the start of the climb for Section 8, the Dragon's Back.

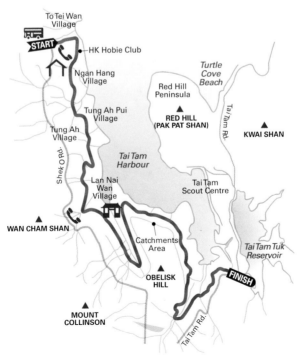

To Tei Wan
Village

START

HK Hobie Club

Ngan Hang
Village

Tung Ah Pui
Village

Tung Ah
Village

Shek O Rd.

WAN CHAM SHAN

Lan Nai
Wan
Village

Red Hill
Peninsula

Turtle
Cove
Beach

RED HILL
(PAK PAT SHAN)

Tai Tam
Harbour

Tai Tam Rd.

KWAI SHAN

Tai Tam
Scout Centre

Catchments
Area

OBELISK
HILL

MOUNT
COLLINSON

Tai Tam Tuk
Reservoir

FINISH

Tai Tam Rd.

Cross the road. A sign says "To Diety Beach". Steps lead downhill, past an overgrown wartime pillbox, to the quiet sands. At the far end, amongst the remains of a village, you'll find the Lam Kee café, which sells cold drinks and hot noodles.

The Hong Kong Hobie Club has its unassuming clubhouse at the other end. The club was established in the late 1970s at Stanley, across the bay, and moved to To Tei Wan a few years later. Today, a fleet of around 70 hobie cats are kept on the dunes. Their seafaring owners are ferried over from Stanley and Tai Tam at weekends, to take part in races and beach parties; on weekdays on the other hand, To Tei Wan feels like it could be located on a desert island. The racing season runs from September to May.

A hiking route follows the coastline north, and gives you a range of views of the harbour. To follow it, return to the steps and turn left at the fork. The path rises slowly, taking you up the hillside above the abandoned villages of Ngan Hang and Tung Ah. (They are best avoided if you are wary of feral dogs).

An ebb tide washed up on the rocks

Making waves across Tai Tam Harbour

Tai Tam Tuk dam retains tons of water

Surfing hero heads for a tumble

Across the water, you're looking at the upscale houses of Redhill. As well as hobies, the surface of the bay is crossed by pleasure junks, speedboats and waterskiers. The Scouts run a sea activity centre for nascent nautical types.

To the north, the great granite dam of the Tai Tam Tuk reservoir spans a valley, while the Stanley peninsula stretches out into the open sea to the south.

Rarely-used paths lead downhill to the coastal villages. Soon, the yellow-roofed temple at Lan Nai Wan can be seen below. Around it lie fishponds and sandy fields, tended to by a dwindling number of farmers. It's a world away from life on the northern shore of Hong Kong Island.

Rarely-used pathway leads to Lan Nai Wan village temple

The harvest of a green-fingered granny

Victorian-era bridge at Tai Tam Tuk

The trail follows a shaded catchwater for its remaining length, meaning flat and easy walking. Look out for tiny, red-clawed crabs which live under fallen leaves. The catchment circles and draws rainwater from Obelisk Hill, named for the stone marker at its peak erected by the Admiralty in Victorian times. Precisely one nautical mile north of a similar obelisk on the same line of longitude, the two were used by the Royal Navy for navigational purposes.

Blue-painted sluice gates mark the end of the catchwater, and the road is not far off. If you have time, you can catch the bus to Stanley for dinner. Turn left upon reaching Tai Tam Road and find the bus stop near the dam. The dam was completed in 1904 and is wide enough for one large vehicle to pass at a time – many rear-view wing mirrors have been lost over the years. Otherwise, cross the road and hop on bus 14 back to the MTR station.

Sluice gates open up to a rush of water after heavy seasonal rains

Peng Chau

2 HOURS

Even compared to Cheung Chau or Lamma, Peng Chau is a tiny island. Sheltering in the lee of mighty Lantau, it faces Discovery Bay but remains a little-visited outpost of island life.

Traditionally it was a fishing settlement, but the islanders diversified into light industry. In the 1940s, the northern part of Peng Chau was home to Southeast Asia's largest match factory, and other enterprises produced furniture, ceramics, leather goods and metal tubing. Remains of the old workshops, and of earlier lime kilns, can still be found scattered around the island. The town's buildings are shabby, even – perhaps especially – the newer ones. But once away from the main street, a variety of heritage sites and viewpoints can be visited.

Pennants flutter for an island festival

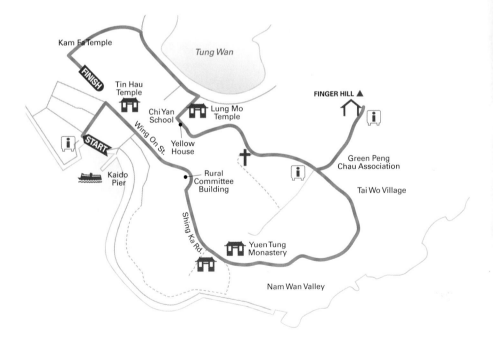

Take the ferry from Central's Pier 6. The journey takes less than an hour by either fast or slow ferry. Leaving the pier, turn right and walk straight ahead, between a line of big old trees, to the island's most prized antiquity, the Tin Hau temple. Its age is not known, but it was restored in 1798. A pair of couplets inscribed inside the temple record the surrender of famous pirate Cheung Po Tsai to the Qing dynasty authorities. There's also a model of an old wooden junk. Each year, the statue of Tin Hau is taken on a procession around the town. The temple was recently damaged by fire but repairs are almost complete.

Outside the temple, a stone tablet dating from 1825 records the islanders' plea for an end to the practice of soldiers hiding in fishing boats to ambush pirates, as it was ruinous to their livelihood. Their request was granted, and this stone was erected to prove the fact.

Park and ride: bikes meet the ferry   *Leafy HQ for rural affairs*

Pass the tablet to walk down Wing On Street, the town's main market alley. Peng Chau has a good range of shops and cafés for such a small island. It once even had a cinema. Some of the buildings are very old, but in poor condition. At the end of the street, take the track which heads uphill, with the yellow house on your left, and then turn right to pass under the archway. At the health centre, carry on up the steps to your left.

At the top of this leafy hill you'll find the old Peng Chau Rural Committee building, a nice old place probably dating from the 1960s if it is the same age as the two pavilions which stand either side of it. Nowadays one half of it is used as a games hall for kids. Bear right to walk around it; from its lawn you have a great view of the coast of Lantau, with the Trappist Monastery (see p.170) perched high up in its steep valley.

Across the clear, deep channel to Lantau

From the far end of the compound, descend by way of green-railed steps to the main track, and turn right to reach a small Taoist temple guarded by stone lions and identified by its yin-yang symbol. Go straight ahead and keep left to pass the decorated yellow-orange gateway of the Yuen Tung Buddhist temple.

Now the long grass takes over and you're well away from the urban world. Below you, the valley of Nam Wan is still firmly agricultural, old village houses set amid orchards and ponds. Passing the columbarium, keep left at the fork to walk through Tai Wo village. At the crossroads with a red sign, go straight ahead –

Gate to Yuen Tung temple

the path drops down into a valley occupied by Happy Farm, an organic venture supported by the Green Peng Chau Association. Healthy eaters can have organic vegetables delivered to their kitchens every week, and weekend gardeners can even rent plots to grow their own produce. The locally-run association has been very active in promoting sustainable living and eco-tourism on Peng Chau.

Well-stocked altar

Returning to the crossroads, turn right to follow the path uphill through the village, bearing right again to reach the hillside path. At the mapboard, take the path which leads up to the top of Finger Hill. It's not particularly high, but from this point you have a wonderful 360-degree view of not only the town below, but of the Western Harbour, Lantau and all the outlying islands.

Village homes in bamboo jungle

Retracing your steps down to the mapboard, turn right and descend back into the town. As you see the church, go straight ahead beside the playground, and then turn right to follow a back lane. Have a look through the gates at Chi Yan School. A pair of palm trees frame its entrance. Built in the 1930s, its stucco porch bears the emblem of the Kuomintang, which was then in power in China.

The south of the island still resides in the past

Dwarfed by Lantau, Peng Chau is a little-visited offshore isle

Rocky shore below organic farms

A few more steps lead you to Tung Wan bay, where the Lung Mo or 'Dragon Mother' temple looks out to sea. It was originally established in Kwai Chung in 1941 but was moved to Peng Chau in 1970. It's well appointed, with dragon sculptures and gleaming gold finery inside. It recalls a woman of ancient times who raised five baby dragons, which in later life returned to protect her from the Emperor.

Goddess of the golden flower

Turn left to walk north along the shore, or what remains of it – residents had to fight to have sand restored to the beach after a bizarre government project to encase the bay in cheap concrete dragged on for years. Turn inland at the pink building and follow the track over a rise. On the other side you'll find a temple to Kam Fa, goddess of the golden flower. The temple is small but brightly painted and is built around a banyan tree. Kam Fa was a girl who secretly learned kung fu from her father, and used it to rob the rich and help the poor, like a Tang dynasty Robin Hood. Beside the temple there is an old well, designed in octagonal shape like a 'bagua' diagram.

Palms frame an old stucco entranceway

The popularity of Kam Fa has surged since the temple was restored from dilapidation in 1978, and although the shrine remains small, it has an army of followers. Even Chris Patten paid a visit. Photos on a noticeboard record the lion dances which take place here every year to celebrate Kam Fa's birthday.

Just below the temple lies the town's main street, and turning left will bring you back to the Tin Hau temple. The ferry pier is straight ahead, with connections to Central and Silvermine Bay. For alternative onward transport, a 'kaido' leaves from the neighbouring public pier for Discovery Bay roughly once an hour until 10:00pm.

Tai Tam Country Park

2 HOURS

It's fortunate for the modern hiker that Hong Kong's early administrators took such care to protect their water supplies. Much of the high land of Hong Kong Island was reserved for a network of water catchments, aqueducts and reservoirs, and as a result escaped development long enough to be included in the country parks system. Although the catchments have long been superseded by gigantic reservoirs in the New Territories, the land they guard remains closed to vehicles and serves as a nature playground for denizens of the city.

Bridge over calm waters

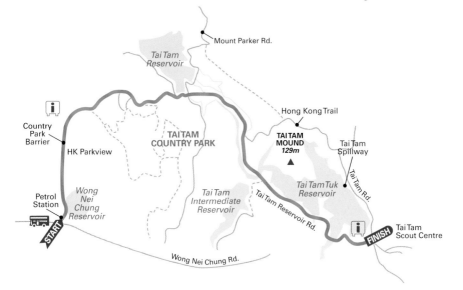

Green gladiators: a lizard claims victory

The largest of Hong Kong Island's green lungs, Tai Tam Country Park, occupies its high eastern massif. Plan a visit after heavy rains, to enjoy the park at its best; rushing water is always a welcome sight on a hot summer's day.

Take Bus No 6, destination Stanley, from the Exchange Square bus terminus. Slow passage through the peopled canyons of Central and Wan Chai soon gives way to a grumbling climb and views over the Happy Valley racecourse. As the bus approaches the pass, you can see the manicured lawns of the Hong Kong Cricket Club on the left. Get off at the next stop.

The cricket club originally occupied the space now known as Chater Garden, but was removed to Wong Nei Chung Gap in the 1970s, when its presence at the heart of the business district became something of a colonial anachronism. Walk past it towards the Shell petrol station, passing the wartime monument to the St. John Ambulance Brigade, and take the steps up to the left. Emerging opposite a set of gilded gates, turn left again and aim uphill for the stone retaining walls of the Wong Nei Chung Reservoir, dated 1899.

There's a café at this reservoir, which is not part of the Tai Tam system. Carp and ducks compete for scraps of bread. Pedal boats rented by the hour are popular with weekend families, who scull their way across the water as casually as the resident terrapins.

Carry on along the road past the Parkview development, cunningly built on land left just outside the country park boundary, and negotiate the black-and-white road barrier. From this point onwards, no vehicular access is allowed, and birdsong takes the place of traffic noise. This track is in fact one of the oldest roads in Hong Kong; it was built in 1847 as the first link between Victoria and Stanley.

Coasting downhill, you pass a Management Centre and Tree Walk before reaching two narrow bridges spanning a neck of the Tai Tam Reservoir. First proposed in the 1870s, and added to as the population relentlessly grew, the three reservoirs were completed by 1918. The blue railings are more reminiscent of an English towpath than anything in the city we have left behind.

A trail to the right follows a catchwater all the way to Repulse Bay. Take the left-hand bridge, cross to the other side and turn right. This brings you past a waterworks building, dated 1904, to a granite spillway. Water cascades down its stone slopes to regain its more natural course below. A tall milestone stands to attention beside the path; look closely and, depending on the light, you may be able to trace the words "Stanley" and "Victoria," and faint Chinese characters, carved into its side. Look behind for a view of the wedding-cake dam holding back the waters of the upper reservoir.

Overflow after seasonal rains

Countless cascades at the height of the rainy season

Moving on downhill, the trees on either side are filled with nesting birds. Barbecue sites attract parties of weekend chefs. Mount Parker Road branches off towards Quarry Bay. Suddenly the parapet of the Tai Tam Intermediate Reservoir is visible high up to the right, waves of white water falling in a regular pattern down its frontage. The path now levels out and you are led over a series of bridges beside the lowest reservoir, Tai Tam Tuk. A village lies drowned beneath its milky-blue surface, floating congregations of wild turtles hovering over what was once farmland. Traffic gingerly crosses the precipitous main dam at its far end.

The third and final bridge is the most picturesque, spanning a calm inlet by way of three granite arches. Shortly afterwards you reach the edge of the country park at Tai Tam Road. Cross over to catch Bus No. 14, or speedier green minibuses, to Stanley. Many buses depart from there for Central.

Spillway of the main reservoir

This hike can be extended by continuing downhill along the path behind the bus stop. Bypassing Hong Kong International School, the track leads to the shore of Tai Tam Harbour, a Victorian-era pumping station and a jetty popular with anglers.

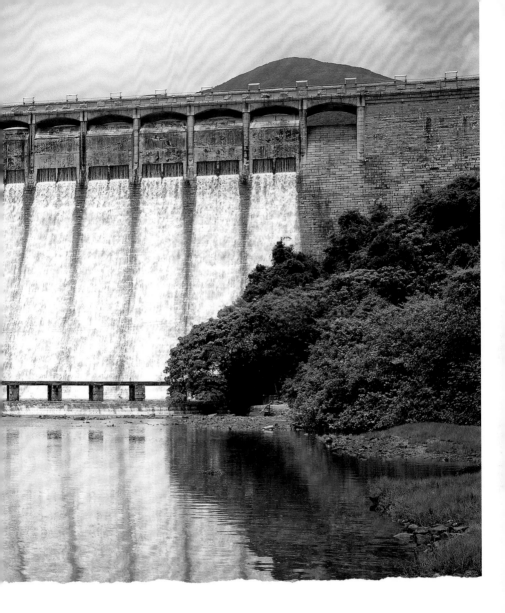

Turning back to follow the shore north, you pass a village café and abandoned statuary before reaching a wide, shallow creek. The high wall of the main dam stands directly above, and during times of rain, vast volumes of water spill over its sides to flood into the pool below. Cross the low bridge and take the steps uphill to reach the bus stop at the north end of the dam.

Cruise liner passing through the Lei Yue Mun strait

Museum of Coastal Defence

1 HOUR

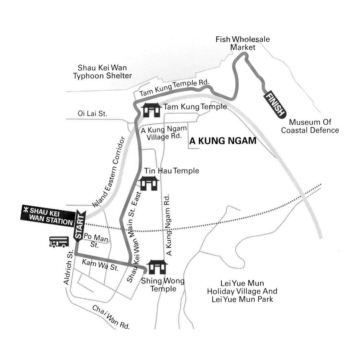

Shau Kei Wan is a working fishing port at the eastern end of Hong Kong Island's built-up area. As well as taking in the Museum of Coastal Defence, this walk includes many temples erected by fisher-folk, and gives you a good idea of a typical old-style working-class district.

Take the MTR to Shau Kei Wan and find your way to Exit A2. Bus 720 from Central also passes this way. You could turn left immediately and head in the direction of the Wellcome supermarket, but we recommend instead a mini detour by crossing the road to the Macau Jockey Club betting shop on the corner directly ahead. Walk past this, turning left into Kam Wa Street.

This street is a busy fruit and fish market, which is especially photogenic in the evenings, when all the stalls are lit by identical red lamps. Women call out the prices of fresh produce, which is attractively laid out on display in bowls or large shallow baskets.

Head past the red minibuses to the tram terminus. This is the eastern end of the tram system, and if you have more time, you might like to arrive in Shau Kei Wan by this mode of transport – it should take around 45 minutes from Central.

A temple to Shing Wong, the city god, lies in a garden on the other side, with attractive paper lanterns hanging from the doorway. After browsing the interior and gardens, return to the tram circle and turn right into Shau Kei Wan Main Street East.

Weighing up fruits of the season   *Ocean's wealth extolled in carved detail*

This road used to be on the old waterfront, and was the commercial heart of the area. It's still packed with local-style shops selling everything from sweets and fried snacks to consumer goods and religious offerings. A short way along you'll find the Tin Hau Temple, open 9:00-5:00 pm, sunk a little lower than the road. It dates from the 1870s. Inside it is black and grimy from decades of incense smoke. Two well-fed cats share residence with a fortune teller. The temple boasts two fierce-looking door gods painted on its main doors to protect it from malevolent spirits.

Door gods on duty

Dragon lady

Coils of incense to appease the gods

Behind the temple, an area of squatter homes has been demolished – leaving the odd sight of angular banyans, which grew around the walls of houses, now standing alone.

Carry on northwards, passing Basel Road, named for the Basel Mission that once operated here. At the next junction, take the subway underground towards the Tam Kung Temple; you can see its green roof tiles ahead.

Like Tin Hau, Tam Kung is another deity popular with seafarers. This temple was built around 1905 and features exceptional interior roof decoration. While here, you can also stroll to the waterfront to take a look at the typhoon shelter. Reclamation has moved it far away from its original location near the MTR. A large fleet of ocean-going fishing ships lies moored near the breakwater, and sampans scuttle back and forth. Hong Kong's fishing industry is not what it was, and nowadays the ships are often confined to port for long periods of time.

Deep-sea trawlers in port for rehabilitation and repair

The canopy-covered redoubt is now the museum

Insurance against French naval ambitions

Follow Tam Kung Temple Road to where a row of tin shipyards lines the left-hand side. Some of these are bustling with workers and visitors. One of them even serves beer! The owners are friendly and will allow you to pass through the docks to view the waterfront.

Just after the Wholesale Fish Market, you can make a short detour over the zebra crossing to see ramshackle Ah Kung Ngam Village, incongruously nestled amongst industrial buildings. 'Ngam' means 'cave' and recalls the many stone quarries that once marked the area. The village has a small but well-attended temple to Yuk Wong (the 'Jade King'), and a maze-like layout of alleys sometimes no more than two feet wide.

Your final stop is the Museum of Coastal Defence, back on the other side of the road, from where you will easily recognize its white canopy strung taut against the blue sky. Opened in 2000, it occupies the grounds and batteries of the old Lei Yue Mun Fort. This cape guarded the eastern approaches to Victoria Harbour, and as such was heavily fortified before the war. A trail leads down to the site of the Brennan Torpedo, an 1890s-era nautical installation which was one of the Victorians' secret weapons, while the central Redoubt has been transformed into an absorbing exhibition gallery recalling the story of Hong Kong's defence. There are great views across the harbour to Devil's Peak on Kowloon side.

Many hours can be spent at the museum, so be sure to leave enough time to explore. The complex closes at 5:00pm, and is open every day except Thursdays. Signposts point the way back to the MTR.

Model of HMS Tamar, 1863-1941

Bird Garden and Flower Market

1 HOUR

Think of North Kowloon and you think of dilapidated tenements, vice dens and the roaring corridor of Nathan Road. But as the urban sprawl passes Boundary Street, it thins out as if to anticipate the garden suburbs of Kowloon Tong. This walk takes you through some quieter parts of the area and includes two well-known attractions.

High density housing for lemon-yellow occupants

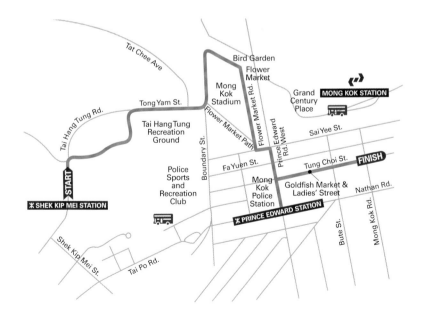

Take the MTR to Shek Kip Mei station on the green line. Leave by Exit B1 and turn right to walk down the hill. This area is typical of a Kowloon public housing estate: dozens of towers providing homes for the working people of the district.

At the first junction, turn right and follow Tong Yam Street down to where it meets the park. This is the Tai Hang Tung Recreation Ground, a wide open area which, exceptionally for our fair city, actually has grass to play on. Families play ball games and groups of teenagers practise their frisbee moves. As you enter the park, turn right and then follow the track which runs the length of the ground. On your right are the fields of the Police Sports Club.

There's a time and place for everything – in moderation

Volleyball practice

Turn left as you emerge onto Boundary Street, so named because this was the limit of British land until the New Territories was acquired in 1898. In fact, if negotiations for the handover of Hong Kong had failed in the early 1980s, then this street would again have become the border in 1997.

Carry on until you can cross over to the other side. You need to walk to the far end of the Mong Kok Stadium, venue of local league football matches, and then turn immediately right. This brings you into the Bird Garden – you can't miss its traditional-style gateway. Besides, it's well signposted by recently installed Tourist Authority directional boards.

One-time border

Kowloon United

Carrying cages for single occupancy songbirds

電話：3942

Relocated from an older part of Mong Kok a few years ago, the Bird Garden is a place for old gents to show off their feathered friends — mynahs, parrots, songbirds and cockatoos among them. Honking traffic noise is swapped for exotic warbling. Stalls sell all kinds of birdkeeping paraphernalia too: crickets and grubs, dainty water bowls and ornate, handmade cages.

Beady eye

Everything a bird lover could desire

As you exit from the far end of the garden, you join the Flower Market, which runs off to the right. This small street is lined from end to end with wholesalers of flowers, shrubs and potted houseplants. It's at its busiest in the very early morning – blooming early, one might say – when trucks load up with blossoms to deliver to florists all over Hong Kong.

It's an early bird market for the best blooms

At the end of Flower Market Road, you have a choice: to return to the MTR, you can turn left and then right, crossing Tung Choi Street, passing the old Mong Kok Police Station on the right which dates from the 1920s. It's hard to believe

Every day at the market is a festival of flowers

that this building must once have overlooked paddy fields. Or, if your legs are still strong, you can turn left to cross Prince Edward Road and then make your way down Tung Choi Street. The colourful Goldfish Market located here on both sides of the road precedes the shopping opportunities of 'Ladies' Street' further on.

Fish in Chinese waters – symbol of harmony and connubial bliss

Cetacean spotters set off from beneath the drawbridge

Dolphin Spotting and Tai O

1.5 HOURS

Formerly the 'capital' of Lantau Island, Tai O is a remote town with a very distinct character. Best known for its stilt houses – tin shacks built on stilts over the creek by Tanka families – it also has numerous sights on land. Its heyday as a fishing port well behind it, moves have recently been made to realize its tourism potential.

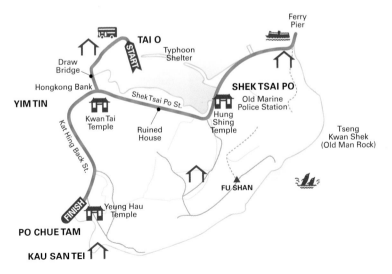

Fishing boats at anchor

Buckets of fresh seafood are the Tai O welcome

Dried fruits of the sea

Take bus 1 from Mui Wo ferry pier or bus 11 from Tung Chung MTR. Each journey takes a good 40-50 minutes, and the terminus is your destination. As you alight from the bus, you'll see a brand-new promenade on your left. This borders the new typhoon shelter for fishing vessels. Beyond it, Tai O's ancient and disused salt pans are being seeded with mangroves, as part-replacement for those lost at the site of the new airport.

From the bus stop, walk straight ahead past the mapboard, turning right onto Tai O Wing On Street. Outside the provisions stores and cafés, tables are set up selling pungent shrimp paste, dried fish, fruit tea and handicrafts. On your right there's an exhibition of local antiquities organized by the Tai O Rural Committee. It's a good collection of relics, photographs and other memorabilia of a time when Tai O was a thriving port. The exhibition hall opens from 12:30pm to 5:00pm every day except Mondays.

Walking on, take the first left. A drawbridge spans the creek, replacing the rope-drawn sampan which formerly did the job. Cross over to the other side. Here, at the water's edge, fibreglass boats offer brief dolphin-spotting tours for $20 per head. Jump aboard!

Your boat will zoom out past the creek's stilt houses, swing around the long ferry pier and enter the flat, open waters of the Pearl River Estuary. After he has switched off the engine, the boatman may point out Old Man's Rock, a stone formation on the coast. A military lookout post tops the hill above it. It's here that you should be able to spot some Chinese White Dolphins, endangered cetaceans commonly known as 'pink dolphins'. The species lives only in this area, apparently liking the mix of salt and fresh water. We saw three dolphins, which seemed to be more white than pink, before skimming back to town.

The trip lasts 20 minutes or so. If there are no boats waiting at the drawbridge when you arrive, you can call Mr Cheung on 9689-8669.

Traditional salt fish is a Hong Kong staple

The tin hut bulletin board announces Cantonese opera

Once a wealthy residence, now a ruin

Hung Shing holding court
Door gods welcome visitors

Bamboo art installation: in dedication to all vertigo-defying scaffolding masters of Hong Kong

Once you're back on dry land, you can take a walk out to the area you've just visited by boat. From the bridge, walk straight ahead, passing HSBC on your right. With its old buildings and milling crowds, this street looks like old Canton or a set from a kung fu movie. Turn left at the top onto Shek Tsai Po Street, passing the vegetable market as you go.

As you walk along the coast, tin shacks line the seaward side of the path while large, balconied buildings line the other. Here public toilets are conveniently located. Take a look at the ruined two-storey house hidden behind a small garden. Its size and posh balustrades suggest a prosperous past.

Further on, the path makes a left-hand turn alongside mud flats. Take a short detour to the right to see the Hung Shing temple, built in 1736. The buildings and grounds of the old Tai O Public School next door are being converted into a 'Shaolin Wushu Culture Centre' to promote martial arts.

Tour boats visit Tai O, but few ferries make the journey

Shoreline blooms brighten Shek Tsai Po

A line of houses beside the water have front gardens – very unusual in Hong Kong. Follow the path through a cluster of humbler houses and small shrines to reach the frontage of the Fish Marketing Organization office. No longer in operation, the land in front is nevertheless still used to dry shrimp paste, spread out on flat rattan baskets. Strangely purple in colour, it is bottled and on sale everywhere in Tai O.

On the hill behind, the former District Office stands empty. Further along, the former Tai O police station also sits in quiet neglect. Painted in the blue and white colours of the Marine Police, it was built in 1902, four years after Britain took control of Lantau Island.

You've reached the old ferry pier. Here, you're closer to Macau than to Central. Once again you may see dolphins emerging from the water some way off the coast.

Picture perfect: the reality is grittier but much more interesting

The police station is silent, its watchtowers blind

Seafront tribute to Marquis Yeung

Retrace your steps. Maybe you'll have noticed that all of Tai O's civic facilities – post office, police station, fire station, clinic – are located along Shek Tsai Po Street. This is because until the 1970s, Tai O had no road connection to the rest of Hong Kong. All visitors entered by sea, by way of the ferry pier. Now that buses arrive on the other side of the creek, and most ferry services have been discontinued, Tai O is in effect facing the wrong way.

Back at the market, you can continue straight ahead, past the Kwan Tai temple onto narrow Kat Hing Back Street. This leads eventually to the picturesque Yeung Hau temple.

Otherwise you can cross the drawbridge to return to Wing On Street. If you turn left here, you can visit another exhibition: the Tai O Culture Workshop at No. 54. Opened by a local woman who has preserved the implements used by generations of fisherfolk, and located on the ground floor of the family house, it is open from 1:00pm to 5:00pm on weekends. It may sometimes open on other days; call 2985-6118 to enquire.

There are restaurants on both sides of the creek. Treat yourself to some local seafood before taking the bus back whence you came – or, as an alternative, take bus 21 or a blue taxi up the mountain to enjoy a vegetarian meal at Po Lin Monastery.

The Kwan Tai temple faces the market

With the escalator through popular SoHo

High West

3 HOURS

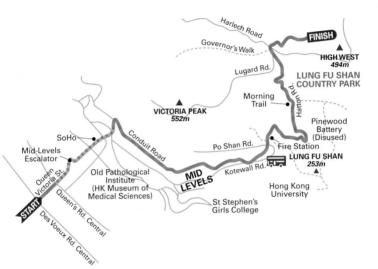

Two spectacular mountains crown the western end of Hong Kong Island. By far the best known is Victoria Peak but, to the dismay of hikers, its summit is closed to the public. On this hike we tackle its neighbour, High West, wild and solitary with views for miles around.

Start off in Central. Take the Mid-Levels escalator past the SoHo area to its terminus on Conduit Road, and turn right. This road, now flanked on either side by multi-storey marble palaces competing for harbour views, began life in 1877 as a humble aqueduct carrying water from Pok Fu Lam to the young city. A long-vanished villa at no. 41 was used as a movie location for

Steering a steady course on a Sunday hike

Rain-swollen waters rush rapidly downstream

Picnic at Pinewood Battery – a wartime relic

"Love is a Many-Splendoured Thing" and served as the then headquarters of the Foreign Correspondents Club. Carry on until Kotewall Road appears on your right. If you want to cut to the chase, this spot can also be reached by bus no. 13 from Edinburgh Place or by green minibus 3A from Central near IFC II.

Hatton Road rises steeply from this point. Walk up to its far end, where vehicle access ends. A small bridge takes you over the fire station on Po Shan Road. Instantly you enter a world of trickling streams and cool forest cover. Handsome banyan trees cling to retaining walls and rock faces, and the din of the city is lost in the canopy of leaves above.

A boundary stone set into the side of the path marks the 1903 boundary of the City of Victoria. Ignore the first right-hand turning but take the second. This track swings around to end amidst the ruins of Pinewood Battery, a wartime fortification superbly situated high above the Western Harbour. Built in 1903 to protect against a feared French or Russian invasion, it instead suffered extensive damage from the Japanese during the Second World War. Hatton Road was in fact built to supply the battery. Today, it's a fine place to

Western district from the heights of High West

enjoy sunsets. Bearing left, make your way to its far side, where you can mount a new flight of steps punctuated by outdoor exercise stations.

Rejoining Hatton Road, it's not long before you reach the open playground where four pedestrian roads meet. This space is usually busy with weekend walkers and picnicking families. Walk straight ahead to find a narrow, tree-shaded path leading south. An open green provides views of Mount Kellett. Then a flight of stairs beckons you up High West.

It's a short but steep trek amongst low scrub up to the airy summit, from which 360-degree views over all of western Hong Kong may be enjoyed. A vast expanse of shimmering water extends to the shores of Lantau. On clear days, distant islands in China can be picked out on the horizon.

A compass board is on hand to point out some of the landmarks.

Return to the playground the same way and turn right onto Harlech Road. This flat, shady stretch leads all the way to the Peak Tower. You can enjoy a meal at any one of the restaurants at this busy tourist site. The Peak tram, bus No. 15 or green minibus No. 1 will carry you back to Central.

The companionship of Sunday hikers

Watchful door gods examine entrants

Ping Shan and the Wetland Park

3.5 HOURS

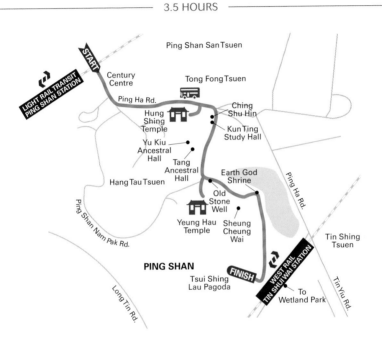

The wealthy Tang clan arrived in what is now known as Hong Kong in the 12th century, and established themselves in various locations in the New Territories. Some of the study halls, temples and ancestral halls they built in Ping Shan are still standing, and a signposted heritage trail makes it easy to see them. This walk also takes in the new Hong Kong Wetland Park, on the other side of Tin Shui Wai new town.

The caveat attached to this route is that the northwest New Territories is a flat alluvial plain, with no mountains for backdrop; and along with the ancient architecture you must also endure the untidy village sprawl and container parks which are a fact of modern New Territories life.

Hung Shing temple: the trail commences

Travel by the KCR's West Rail to Yuen Long station, and change to the LRT light rail system by following the signs through Sun Yuen Long Plaza to ground level. Any departing carriage will do. Alternatively, take bus 968 from outside Pacific Place and sit upstairs – the bus travels through three major tunnels and across the impressive Ting Kau Bridge, and en route you get to see shipyards, container terminals, looped-up noodles of flyovers and ranks of shiny imported cars arranged like Dinky toys far below: a fast-forward DVD of Hong Kong at work. At the Yuen Long bus terminus, backtrack to Castle Peak Road, where you should bear right to cross over to the far platform of the LRT via footbridge.

To travel on the light rail, you must first press your Octopus card against a processor on the platform, and then do the same as you leave. Alight at Ping Shan, which is either five or two stops down the line, depending on which arrival route you choose. Walk ahead and turn right to cross the tracks, then turn immediately left and right again to find Ping Ha Road.

The road curves around to the left to reach Hang Mei Tsuen village. Cross the village square here to see the first item on the trail: the Hung Shing temple, built in 1767. Hung Shing is popular with fishermen and has traditionally had a strong following in Hong Kong. The temple was renovated in 1963, but the materials used have aged well and the building feels old. It is unusual in that it has an open courtyard inside. In the separate hall next door, there is a colourful bas-relief of the 'three star gods' of health, wealth and longevity.

Return to the road and walk past the bus stop to the right-hand turning into the village. Here you'll find Ching Shu Hin – a walled guesthouse built to accommodate visiting Qing-dynasty scholars and officials – and next to it, the Kun Ting Study Hall. The hall was used to educate sons of the clan, and to prepare them for taking the imperial civil service examinations; if a student did well in the exams, he could become a mandarin and

Follow the flowers

bring great prestige to his family. The examination system was done away with in 1904, just seven years before the Qing court met its end.

Further on, the path opens up onto a market square bordered by two imposing buildings: the Tang Ancestral Hall and the Yu Kiu Ancestral Hall. Both are laid out in the same manner, with three halls and two courtyards, although the Tang hall is the older of the two, dating back to the 1300s. Each contains an altar bearing ancestral tablets, along with granite columns and fine roof decorations. The Yu Kiu hall was used as a village school until the 1960s, but it has now been restored and returned to its original purpose.

Grand dimensions: the ancestral halls

Protective gate tower

Village in bloom

Attending to earth gods

Carrying on north, you can go straight ahead at the crossroads to visit a very simple Yeung Hau temple, dedicated to Hau Wong. An inscription inside records that it was renovated in the 52nd year of the Chinese republic, i.e. 1963, the same year that the Hung Shing temple was repaired. Return to the signpost and turn right – you'll pass an old stone well before arriving at the entrance to Sheung Cheung Wai, a traditional walled village which still retains its grey-brick gatetower. Step inside and you'll see that the layout of the village is perfectly symmetrical, with a central shrine at the far end.

Beyond the village, there is an earth god shrine beside old fishponds. Turn right here and follow the road directly ahead, past the college building, until it mounts a rise. Down on your right is the attractive Tsui Shing Lau pagoda, a hexagonal three-storey tower. Built over 600 years ago, it is Hong Kong's only ancient pagoda. It was probably built for feng shui purposes, possibly to prevent flooding, as Ping Shan then sat on the edge of an estuary; but a deity housed on the top floor was also believed to bestow success or failure in examinations. The pagoda has spent much of the past 20 years surrounded by breakers' yards, although the land around it is now used much more suitably by Japanese-style barbecue restaurants. Amazingly, Tsui Shing Lau was only declared a protected monument in 2001.

Tsui Shing Lau: the Pagoda of Gathering Stars

You can enter the pagoda to view a small exhibition of local history. It's open from 9:00am to 5:00pm but is closed on Tuesdays.

Take the steps up now behind the pagoda to once again find the LRT platform. Take train 706, a circular service which rings the far-flung new town of Tin Shui Wai, and alight after 10-15 minutes at the Wetland Park station. Cross the footbridge and then bear left to reach the entrance to the park.

Native white egrets

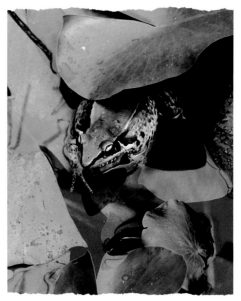
Amphibious pond life

Under the boardwalk: a watery habitat

Blossoms after rain

Fragile visitor

Opened in 2006, the 60-hectare Wetland Park aims to showcase the diversity of Hong Kong's wetland ecosystems, and inform the public of the need to conserve them. Boardwalks and hides allow visitors to see mangroves, fishponds and mudflats, and the species of aquatic and bird life which live in these habitats. A special enclosure is home to Pui Pui, the famous Yuen Long crocodile who evaded capture for so long. In addition, there is an indoor 'interactive world' with themed exhibition galleries. There's quite a lot to see. The Wetland Park has been flooded with an unforeseen volume of visitors since its opening, and it's a good idea to avoid going there at weekends, when herds of people deter flocks of birds. The park is open from 10:00am to 5:00pm every day except Tuesday – but beware, the last visitor is admitted at 4:00pm. Admission is $30 for adults and $15 for kids.

Duly educated in the world of water, jump back on the 706; it will take you to the Tin Shui Wai West Rail station, where you can catch a train back to Kowloon. Cross-harbour buses 967 and 969 also run from Tin Shui Wai back to Hong Kong Island. Alternatively, if hunger pangs are imminent, flag down a green cab for a $20 taxi ride to Lau Fau Shan – a fishing town on the edge of Deep Bay which is well known for its oysters and seafood restaurants.

In the event that you are bitten by a snake – which is unlikely because the snake would rather get out of your way – experts caution against sucking out the venom.

Your best course is to stay calm and avoid unnecessary movement. Rapid body motion only accelerates the venom's circulation in your bloodstream.

Firmly bandage the area above the bite and head for the nearest hospital as soon as possible. All Hong Kong hospitals stock anti-venom for snakes commonly found in the territory.

If you can't deliver the remains of the reptile – which may be a protected species – try to provide a full and accurate description, with particular attention to markings and coloration, so doctors can choose the right anti-venom.

Every year some 200 people in Hong Kong receive treatment for snakebites, none of which have proved fatal since records were kept.

While you shouldn't underestimate the danger, you shouldn't overestimate it either. The majority of snakes are harmless to humans and more alarmed by an accidental encounter than you might be – for good reason, because many are needlessly destroyed through ignorance.

If you should come across a snake in an urban area you can do it a good turn by calling snake expert Dave Willot at 2328-2526. He is dedicated to saving snakes from the consequences of ophidiophobia (fear of snakes).

Fallen soldiers of World War Two

Sai Wan War Cemetery

2 HOURS

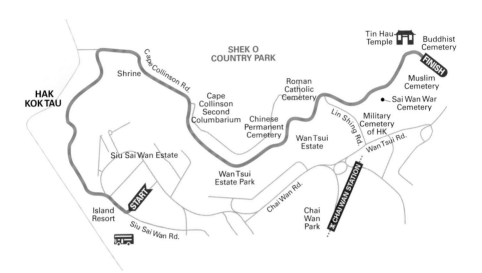

The hills around Chai Wan are blanketed with numerous cemeteries – Chinese, Catholic, Buddhist and Muslim. Amongst them lies a burial ground for Commonwealth soldiers who lost their lives defending Hong Kong. This walk makes a circuit of these hillsides. One word of warning: avoid the Ching Ming and Chung Yeung grave-sweeping festivals, when the cemeteries are crowded with visitors and the narrow roads are jammed with honking taxis.

Leafy suburb: Heng Fa Chuen

Take the MTR's Island Line to Heng Fa Chuen and leave by exit A2. Turn right, descend the steps and walk along to the minibus stand. Jump on minibus 62A, or into a taxi, for the short hop to Island Resort in Siu Sai Wan. On arrival, walk through the bus station to the nicely laid out waterfront.

Turn right to follow the boardwalk. Signboards have been erected to explain the view: Junk Island, site of an imperial Chinese customs house, is across the bay.

The boardwalk ends at a public park, and it's easy to find the steps leading uphill at the far end, lined by new metal railings. A government sign declares that dogs must keep to the yellow-brick path as they pass through the park – it seems almost redundant to point out that not only are dogs unable to read, but they are also colour-blind!

The steps meet a junction. Take either way, as both eventually lead up to a sitting-out area. Cross the blue-fenced bridge to reach the main paved trail, which climbs gently uphill. It's a quiet road with no traffic, popular with morning walkers and strolling families alike. Disused telegraph poles are half hidden amongst the trees; perhaps they once carried messages over the hill to the lighthouse at Cape Collinson. The beacon still stands on what is still a very rugged coastline, but it is visible only from the seaward side.

Sea views fit for millionaires at Island Resort

The track travels steadily south to meet Cape Collinson Road at a pleasantly shaded spot. Morning walkers have erected shrines and makeshift shelters under the trees. Left from here, at the end of a road lined with wartime bunkers, lies the grim Cape Collinson Correctional Institute – isolated from the rest of Hong Kong Island like the lighthouse further north. You should turn right.

Harbour traffic, big and small

Verdant frame for a view of the Tathong Channel

Weekend walkers pause at Cape Collinson

Chinese cemeteries extend up and along the hillside on your left, while public housing estates occupy the former bay below. It's a level walk. Eventually, passing Wan Tsui Estate Park on the right and a cluster of shanty homes housing stonemasons on the left, you reach a junction with Lin Shing Road. Go straight ahead and carry on uphill.

The Hong Kong Military Cemetery appears shortly on your right. This is a Christian burial ground for members of Hong Kong's armed forces. The main Sai Wan War Cemetery, which honours those who fell during the Second World War, is a little further up the road.

The Sai Wan Memorial, with its two square openings, is the entrance to the cemetery. The names of over 2000 Commonwealth soldiers are engraved on the slabs of Portland stone, but the cemetery contains the remains of only around 1600; many men who died in the Battle of Hong Kong, or in prisoner-of-war camps, have no known grave. The cemetery, which is maintained by the Commonwealth War Graves Commission, descends in terraces towards the sea.

Siu Sai Wan sprouts up along the shore

The Pacific War is brought to life for a party of schoolchildren

SAI·WAN·WAR·CEMETERY

1939   1945

Regimented stones, some with names and some without

Just up the road, an opening in the fence leads into the neighbouring Muslim Cemetery. Take the steps downhill. Gravestones here bear inscriptions in Chinese, Roman and Arabic scripts.

Blue-domed beacon for Friday prayers

At the foot of the steps you approach the blue-domed Chai Wan Mosque, built in 1963 and one of five in Hong Kong. Friday is the busy day here. Turn right to walk around it, descending a set of steps to its forecourt. A spray of bougainvillea on the right marks your way back downhill.

The path follows a stream alongside the foundations of old squatter villages, finally passing under two curtains of aerial banyan roots to emerge beside a ramshackle Tin Hau temple.

Floral tributes

A tin shed next door houses the Chai Wan Hawkers' Committee. Do hawkers meet here to fix the prices of fishball noodles, or swap intelligence on the movements of anti-hawker patrols? No – perhaps they just play mahjong.

Turn right to follow the road to the junction, and then cross over to enter Hing Wah Shopping Centre. Signs point your way to Chai Wan MTR station.

Tai Po Market and the Railway Museum

2 HOURS

When Britain took charge of the New Territories in 1898, the small market settlement of Tai Po became the centre of administration for the area. Today's new town still hides some vestiges of its Victorian past.

The uniquely Chinese design of the old Tai Po Railway Station

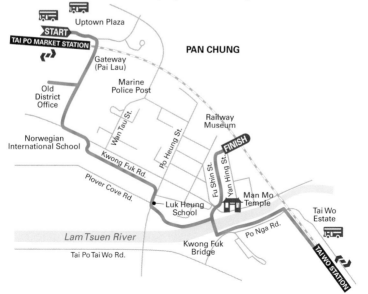

Pai Lau gateway to the family park

Take the KCR to Tai Po Market station, leaving by the exit for Uptown Plaza. Bear right and follow the covered walkway past the private estate buses. A couple of metres further along beware not to miss the underpass beneath the railway line: turn right and up the other side.

A traditional 'pai lau' gateway, dated 1953, bids you welcome to Tai Po Primary School. The school is long gone, but its grounds have been transformed into pleasure gardens. Mature residents perform tai chi exercises under mature trees.

Conservation offices of another era

Passing the football courts, follow the track as it rises uphill to the junction. The old pitched-roof buildings below on the left are now used as offices for the government's conservation section. Stay on this road but turn right onto Wan Tau Kok Lane and carry on uphill, bearing right past the school entrance to the very top.

The elegant colonial structure cresting the hill is the old District Office. Dating from 1907, the red-brick building has cooling verandahs along two sides. All the early development of the northern New Territories — railways, roads and reservoirs — was planned from here. It remained in use until 1983, and is now occupied by the Scouts Association.

Return downhill to where the road bends left. The handsome buildings in the compound ahead were the very first police headquarters built in the New Territories, in 1899. They are currently used as temporary accommodation for the Marine Police. Turn right here between two imposing lemon-scented Eucalyptus gum trees to descend to Kwong Fuk Road by way of the tree-shaded stairway.

Before the arrival of the New Town and the Tolo Highway, Kwong Fuk Road used to be the main thoroughfare of Tai Po — a continuation of the Tai Po Road, which wound its way around the hillside from Sha Tin. Carefully cross the road, as it's a major thoroughfare, and continue on the opposite pavement walking left. Or better still, use the underpass further down Kwong Fuk Road.

Another hidden gem is located on the hill above Groom's Cottage a little further on your right: the old Tai Po Bungalow is now occupied by the Norwegian International School.

The cycle of life: from father to son

Man Sze Cheung Yuen, the balconied art-deco house on the corner, wouldn't look out of place in a 1960s kung fu movie. The house has an unusually large garden behind, full of trees. Carry on along Kwong Fuk Road and take the next right, then proceed down the first alley on your left. This sets you on Luk Heung Lane, which was peopled with villagers displaced by the construction of the Plover Cove reservoir in the 1960s.

The lane, now void of cars, hosts bars, bike rental shops, dai pai dongs and clothes stalls — a typical New Territories back street. Walk to the end, then turn right and at the next set of traffic lights cross the busy road to the Luk Heung School, descending right to reach the Lam Tsuen River promenade. Follow it to the left.

Caucasian models tempt an Asian market.

Former sampan dwellers are now high-rise occupants

Today, this is a carefully channelled river. Try to imagine it in the early years of the last century, when thousands of boat people lived on sampans along the shore.

The red pillared Kwong Fuk Bridge

Soon you reach the green-tiled Kwong Fuk Bridge, built in 1957 according to an inscription on the stone balustrade. It's a 'dual carriageway' crossing — bicycles on one side and pedestrians on the other — but does not cater to cars. Don't cross the bridge, but remain on this shore. Walk down the road between the trees to the traffic junction at Kwong Fuk Road and cross it to enter a van parking area. At this juncture with Po Yik Street you're getting close, as the Tourism Board signposts clearly point you in the direction of the Man Mo Temple and the Railway Museum. Turning left at the first lane brings you onto Fu Shin Street: a classic example of an old street market. All manner of fresh produce are noisily bought and sold. Old-style shops offer traditional sweets and religious paraphernalia.

Halfway down the street you'll find the Man Mo Temple, set in a small garden. Unspoilt by restoration, it looks its age. It's certainly worth a brief visit. Then continue to the end of the street and turn right: the Railway Museum awaits you straight ahead.

Incense coils of amber in a haze of blue

Man Mo Temple, dedicated to two gods: one of literature, the other of war

Built in 1913 as the railway station for Tai Po, it was the only station on the KCR line designed in Chinese style. It has been out of use since electrification of the line in 1983, and now serves as an open-air museum.

You can board old carriages, wander through the ticket office and see the old steam locomotive. The museum is open until 5:00 pm every day except Tuesday.

Return to the modern-day KCR over the river by crossing that 'dual carriageway' Kwong Fuk Bridge, turning left, downhill and walking along Po Nga Road. Follow the signs to the new Tai Wo station.

Kowloon-Canton Railway: British Section, opened October 1910

On a Sunday outing, kids go off the rails

North Lamma

2 HOURS

Hiking the undulating spine of Lamma Island is a popular weekend ritual for expats and locals alike. While attractive in many ways, the sheer number of visitors on a Sunday can taint one's enjoyment of places along the way, and the ferries on weekends are crowded too. Try this alternative route to experience the peace of the island's sparsely inhabited northern terrain while still ending up with a choice of tempting restaurants for dinner.

The fleet, packed like sardines in Aberdeen Harbour

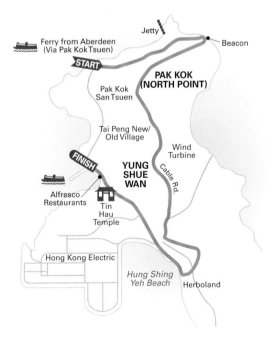

The alternatives start with transport to the island. Instead of taking the usual ferry from Central, we depart from Aberdeen. To get there, take bus 70 from Exchange Square. If you recognize the Aberdeen waterfront, by all means alight when you see it. Otherwise, wait until your bus comes to a stop at the terminus, and then follow the underpass to the waterfront promenade.

Bear right when you meet the water. The gangplank to the ferry can be found a little further on. Look for the modern vessel which goes to Yung Shue Wan – don't confuse it with the older wooden boat which travels to Sok Kwu Wan, or the smaller launches which shuttle to and from the floating restaurants.

Ferries depart roughly once every two hours. The journey costs $12, and it's cash only – if you ask whether Octopus is available, you're likely to be directed to the nearby fish market.

As you leave the harbour, you get a close-up view of varied waterborne lifestyles: old women on sampans, dogs guarding fishing boats and sunbathing day trippers on junks from the marina. The ferry crosses the Lamma Channel, weaving in and out of the wash of gigantic container ships laden with heavy cargo. Get off at the first stop: Pak Kok village.

Suburban Lamma in full bloom

Walk up the path from the pier, bearing left to pass the two village shops. This is your last chance to buy refreshments. As you leave the shops behind to approach overgrown fields, the tranquillity of the area becomes immediately apparent. The village lands are no longer farmed in any significant way, and the scattered houses are home to a small number of commuters who prefer the peace of Pak Kok to the more boisterous nature of Yung Shue Wan along the coast.

Residential high-rises of Aberdeen now engulf the fishing fleet and its ferries

Tricky docking in rough seas at Pak Kok

East Lamma channel divides two worlds

The peaceful 'cable road' never experiences traffic

Keep to the path as it follows a route parallel to the shore, rising and passing through a larger cluster of houses. At the next bay, ignore the turning to the jetty and instead plough straight ahead across the fields, making a right turn to reach a flat area on the opposite side of the headland.

There's a shipping beacon here and views over to Cyberport and Pokfulam. 'Pak Kok' means 'north point' and this is the northernmost tip of Lamma Island. From here you need to turn around and head directly uphill on a wide, paved track.

This 'cable road' was built by Hong Kong Electric in the early 1970s to serve its power station at Yung Shue Wan. Looking back across the channel, you can see the large housing estate of South Horizons on Ap Lei Chau; this was the original site of the power station until the value of that land was realized. This road carries no vehicular traffic and very few walkers either. It's an easy route to follow.

After some time, the track rises high enough to lose its cover of trees, and you're treated to views of Yung Shue Wan below. At the road's highest point, it levels out for a short stretch, and an outcrop on the right provides better views of the whole valley and the coast beyond. Up on your left, Hong Kong Electric's experimental new wind turbine aims to catch the breeze.

Follow the road downhill and turn left where it forks, onto a short track joining the two cable roads, and then make a right turn to carry on downhill. Very soon the road crosses the main island path, and you'll

Wind of change: new power on the horizon

Yung Shue Wan luxuriates down in the valley, served by its very own pier

see swimmers, dog walkers and buggy-pushing parents going in both directions. Turn left for Hung Shing Yeh beach, but then take the first left again to pass through the hillside village of the same name. This gives you the opportunity to check out the pigeon restaurant, a well-known local venue with a nice terrace.

Seafood galore alfresco

The path winds its way across and down to the far end of the beach, where a plot of abandoned farmland has been developed into 'Herboland': an organic farm and open-air café. Stop off for a cup of flower or herb-based tea, and you can watch the resident cats roll around the catnip bush. The farm delivers organic veggies to health-conscious consumers all over Lamma.

Fishermen's festive flags

Cross the beach and follow the hordes of visitors along the well-trodden path into Yung Shue Wan, where you can end your walk with dinner and drinks at any one of a score of restaurants. But don't get too merry to forget the ferry – the last boat for Central leaves at 11:30pm.

Park, pedal and ride

Edwardian survivor on Nathan Road

Monuments of TST

2 HOURS

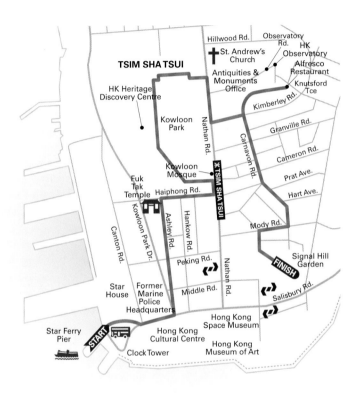

Tsim Sha Tsui is the epitome of a bustling downtown district where time is money and space is in short supply. It's not surprising that many of its most beautiful buildings have fallen to the busy wrecker's ball and been redeveloped many times over – but enough remain to warrant a heritage hike through its noisy, jostling streets.

Take the Star Ferry from Central or Wanchai to the Tsim Sha Tsui pier. The service was initiated in 1888 by Dorabjee Nowrojee, a Parsee businessman who was accustomed to taking friends over to Kowloon on his private launch. The distinctive double-ended vessels have made the back-and-forth journey ever since, although the shore of Hong Kong Island has crept closer with each passing decade. Originally set at just five cents, the fare today is still only $2.20, a great bargain by any measure.

As you exit the pier, the clock tower of the former Kowloon-Canton railway terminus stands on your right. Completed in 1916, it marked the start of epic train journeys across China and Russia to Europe, an alternative to the usual passage by ship. The rest of the station was demolished in 1975 and moved to Hung Hom; in recent years, the area has experienced major disruption thanks to the KCR extending its lines back to Tsim Sha Tsui again.

Asia's World City: the 'Brand HK' Star Ferry docks at TST

The clock tower marks the original terminus of the KCR

Fresh fruit on Haiphong Road

Keeping to the left of the bus terminus, skirt the frontage of Star House – dodging tailors' touts and leaflet wallahs – to cross Canton Road at its end. On the bluff above, the former Marine Police Headquarters is finally undergoing renovation to start a new life as a boutique hotel. The 1880s-vintage building has lain empty since the Marine Police moved out in 1997.

Carry on along Salisbury Road. The red brick house on your left was Tsim Sha Tsui's first fire station, built in 1920. Follow the underpass to emerge beside the YMCA, and turn left, crossing Middle Road and Peking Road to follow Ashley Road north. The street is full of restaurants. It's also a dead end, but you can take the steps at the top to pass through to Haiphong Road. Turn left.

Seeking godly guidance

The 'temporary market' on Haiphong Road has been in situ for around 30 years, since the stallholders were ejected from the Victorian brick marketplace on Peking Road. Down an alley to its left, you'll find the tiny Fuk Tak temple, dedicated mainly to earth gods. Strangely, and despite the fact that this part of Kowloon has been intensively inhabited since the mid-1800s, it is Tsim Sha Tsui's only Chinese temple.

The former Marine Police HQ is a model of tropical colonial design

Turn back now and walk down Haiphong Road to its junction with thunderous Nathan Road, turning left to cross over to the MTR entrance. The Kowloon Mosque here was built in 1984, and is the largest of its kind in Hong Kong. There has been a mosque on this site ever since the British Army stationed Indian soldiers at Whitfield Barracks on the hills behind. The extensive military lands were handed over to the Hong Kong government in 1967, to become today's Kowloon Park.

Crenellated dome of Kowloon Mosque

If you take the steps up into the park, you can make a quick tour of the Health Education Exhibition and Resource Centre on the left; housed in an old army building, its exhibits are aimed mainly at schoolchildren but it has a few items of interest. One area looks at the founding of the Sanitary Board, which became the Urban Council. It's open on Tuesdays, Wednesdays, Fridays and Saturdays from 8.45am-6.15pm, and on Sundays from 11:00am-9:00pm.

Universal park life

Entering the park, turn right to walk uphill, with the ornamental lake on your left. You soon reach the recently opened Hong Kong Heritage Discovery Centre. It's located in the barrack buildings which housed the Hong Kong Museum of History from 1983 to 1998, but they have been carefully restored and look much better than they did before. The centre holds rotating exhibitions of local heritage – one recent display was a trove of archaeological discoveries which had been unearthed during road construction in Sai Kung. It's open from 10:00am-6:00pm, and until 7:00pm on Sundays. Closed Thursdays.

There are other military relics in the park: several pill boxes can be spied hidden amidst the shrubbery, and an old gun position behind the aviary is now used as a lookout point. The park is a nice place for a wander, with flamingo ponds, a hedge maze and a sculpture garden.

Moving on past the Heritage Centre to the circular fountain, turn right to take the walkway over the outdoor swimming pools. The open plaza here hosts an arts fair on Sundays from 1:00-7:00pm. Go straight ahead to descend to the Park Lane Shoppers' Boulevard on Nathan Road. This stretch of pavement is lined with great old trees which would be very welcome on other roads in Hong Kong.

Attentively restored, the Heritage Discovery Centre is as good as new

Restful refuge: Chinese garden in Kowloon Park

Cross the road and bear left. Set on a stone platform, the old Kowloon British School now houses the government's Antiquities and Monuments Office. Built in 1902, the school was intended for the children of expatriates who cautiously began to set up home in Kowloon after the area's reputation as a den of villains and rogues began to wane in the late 1800s.

Behind it, St. Andrew's Church dates from the same era. It was built in 1906 with a donation from Sir Catchick Paul Chater, the entrepreneur who also set up the wharves and godowns on Tsim Sha Tsui's western shore. The company which operates that area – now occupied by Ocean Terminal and Harbour City – is still called Wharf Holdings.

Further back from the road, the Victorian premises of the Hong Kong Observatory are hidden behind lush greenery on a small rise. The

Victorian verandahs at the Hong Kong Observatory

observatory was set up in 1883 to provide typhoon and weather warnings to ships in the harbour. From 1907 to 1933, the observatory operated a signal tower on Blackhead Point, closer to the harbour. A copper ball was dropped from the top of the tower every day at 1:00pm, allowing ships' captains to synchronize their timepieces.

You can still visit the signal tower: it's located in a small garden on Minden Row, just off Mody Road. The observatory's verandahed premises on the other hand are still in daily use, and are not generally open to the public.

Walk back to the pedestrian crossing and turn left onto Kimberley Road. Opposite Carnarvon Road, a turning on your left leads up to Knutsford Terrace, a line of popular restaurants offering alfresco dining. Enjoy dinner or drinks before heading back down Nathan Road to the MTR.

Kowloon's British School

Signal tower on Minden Row

Maritime Museum and CSD Museum

1 HOUR

Two museums – one little known, the other brand new – can be visited on this easy amble through Stanley, a relaxed town on Hong Kong's southside.

The verandahs of Murray House now look out over Stanley Bay

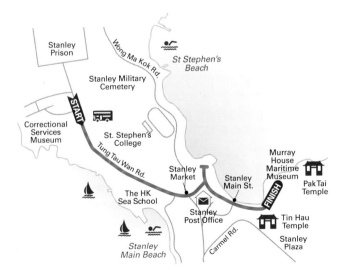

From Exchange Square in Central, board buses 6, 6X or 260. Instead of alighting at the Stanley Market bus station with the other daytrippers, stay on board until the bus reaches its terminus – at the gates of Stanley Prison.

The Hong Kong Correctional Services Museum stands right next to the jail. Admission is free, and they do let you out afterwards, so do go in. Exhibition galleries detail the development of Hong Kong's penal system since the earliest colonial times. Some of the exhibits, such as the flogging rack, may make your eyes water. Beside a replica cell, a description of the sequence of events leading up to the gallows is rather compelling. A Victorian guard's log book records, in flowing hand, the lesser punishments visited upon unruly prisoners.

Stark, stiff and formal, prison warders of the 1920s

Other galleries trace the more recent history of the Vietnamese boat people in Hong Kong. Outside, an annex block displays items made by modern prisoners. There's a nice view of the bay.

Returning to Tung Tau Wan Road, turn right and walk past the Hong Kong Sea School, a training institute for sea cadets. The school occupies large grounds leading down to the beach, and this original building was opened by King Baudouin of Belgium in 1964. Carry on towards the junction with Wong Ma Kok Road, and cross over.

Locked in public punishment

Place of learning for young sea cadets

The neoclassical elegance of Murray House in its new Stanley surrounds

Eating and drinking

Stanley's tiny Post Office stands on your left. Look closely, and you'll see that one of its windows is engraved with a royal 'GR' crest. Take the street which leads steeply downhill beside it, and turn right at the bottom. You're in the heart of the warren which is Stanley Market, with shops and stalls hawking all manner of tourist-oriented art and clothing. Passages and steps lead off in random directions; one goes to the ancient kaifong (neighbourhood association) building.

Make your way to the far end of the alley – which is actually called Stanley Main Street, an indication of the town's labyrinthine nature – and you'll emerge onto the waterfront restaurant strip. The beach has been reclaimed

Shopping in the market – the dilemma of choice

but, today, a more sane policy of outdoor dining is being trialled. By the time you read this, a boardwalk may grace the shore. Walk on, passing Stanley's dragonboat association HQ. The colonnaded edifice of Murray House is your destination.

The Maritime Museum occupies the ground floor of this colonial pile, which used to stand on the site of the Bank of China in Central. Admission is $20. It's a fine place to learn about the story of seafarers on the South China coast. Exhibits span the range of nautical history, from ancient trading routes to modern vessels.

One of several waterfront shrines

Outside, note the stone columns inscribed with Chinese characters. Like Murray House, they were rescued from demolition in the city – in their case, from old shophouses in Mongkok. Nearby, Stanley's Tin Hau temple displays a tiger pelt from an animal which reportedly terrorized the village during the 1940s.

Behind Murray House, take a signposted path that leads along the shore. It ends at a tiny temple to Pak Tai, perched above the rocks.

Backtrack to the restaurants for an alfresco evening meal. Both of Stanley's museums are closed on Mondays.

Bounded by water: you're never far from the sea on Cheung Chau

Old Cheung Chau

2 HOURS

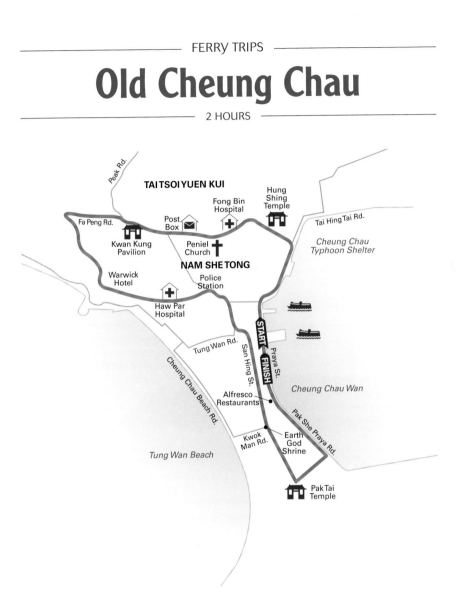

Tiny Cheung Chau is home to many more people than all the other outlying islands put together, and yet more of its built heritage has survived. The tightly packed central area is a good place for spotting antiquities – and that means residents as well as buildings.

Take the ferry from the piers in Central. Arriving on Cheung Chau, turn right and make your way along the praya, past the bunting of outdoor restaurants. At the 'Y' juncture bear right to the municipal services building. Bicycles parked against waterfront railings are matched by sampans moored on the other side.

Salty air, rusty sign

Shortly a shaded plaza appears on your left, occupied by tables from restaurants like Coffee & Tea. Above the far end of the square, you can see the Hung Shing temple, perched on a rise and half-hidden by shopfronts. It's directly behind the Cheung Chau Pig Raising Co-op. Reach it by taking steps up between a stonemason and a street café, and turning at the rusty old street sign. The beautifully maintained temple was built in 1813.

The Hung Shing temple overlooks the harbour

Older buildings open a window into the past

Georgian relic still in use

Leaving by the other end of the temple compound, a hotchpotch of potted plants, drying clothes and delivery trolleys leads to the gateway of the crumbling Fong Bin Hospital. Funded by charitable donations and supported by Lai Chun-bin, a general of the Ching navy, it was established in 1878, twenty years before the island passed into British hands. Lacking medical facilities, it operated as a hospice for the poor. An outbuilding on the slope beside it dates from the 36th year of the Chinese Republic, i.e. 1947.

The busier building behind the hospital is the local Shun Tak District Association. Many Hong Kong residents trace their ancestry to towns or villages in other parts of Guangdong, such as Shun Tak. Follow the path downhill to leave the compound by another sand-coloured archway. Cheung Chau's second-hand bookshop stands opposite. Turn right and pass the whitewashed battlements of Peniel Church to reach School Road. Note the green postbox with its 'GR' crest.

Climb the steps between schools, and at the top pass through black iron gates to enter the well-kept gardens of the Kwan Kung Pavilion. It's not particularly old, having been built in 1973, but keeps to a traditional Taoist style. It is dedicated to Kwan Ti, the red-faced god of war and righteousness. A two-metre long 'dragon bone' is on display in a glass case – it is meant to have been discovered by local fishermen.

Return to the gates and turn left onto Peak Road. Access to this area was once restricted in an effort to develop an exclusive residential district like The Peak on Hong Kong Island. Houses here are noticeably grander and more individual: one wall is decorated with gryphon motifs. Boundary stones were laid to mark the restricted area, and one surviving example is hidden in the grounds of the house at no.1A.

Turn left at the festoon of signposts onto Fa Peng Road, and pass by the island's sports ground (with public toilet facilities if in need). The next double junction, between an abandoned school and a house blessed with a canopy of bougainvillea, is another comical confusion of colourful signage. One sign even points the way 'with the compliments of Hang Lung Bank', an institution which went bust during the currency crisis of the early 1980s.

War and righteousness in Cheung Chau: the Kwan Kung Pavilion

Medical facility built with Tiger Balm money

You need to double back to mount Cheung Chau Sports Road, which rises above the exercise ground. At the end, turn right to pass a green and white pavilion. The road descends around the back of the Warwick Hotel towards the coast.

The building ahead on the left is the Haw Par Hospital, run by the St John Ambulance Association. Walk around its perimeter, bearing left, to reach the entrance. It's a beautiful colonnaded building dating from the 1930s. There is a bust of the founder Aw Boon Haw in the lobby, and it's worth reading the touching inscription recorded on behalf of the grateful villagers. Born in Rangoon, Aw Boon Haw made his fortune from the manufacture of tiger balm ointment. He was a great philanthropist and built the famous Tiger Balm Gardens as well as hospitals and schools in China.

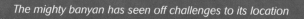
The mighty banyan has seen off challenges to its location

As you leave, turn left uphill and then bear right. A small cannon guards the island's police station, another little-known colonial building dating from 1913.

Turn right going downhill again, along the immaculately swept Police Station Path, and make a left turn onto Tung Wan Road, busy with beachgoers. As the road opens up onto a square, head for the venerable banyan. Rather than chop this tree down to allow passage for Cheung Chau's tiny fire engine, the buildings opposite were demolished instead.

Turn right here into San Hing Street. Shops on either side of this narrow alley sell everything an island resident might need. Older trades like herbalists and chandlers (ships' outfitters) survive amongst the bakeries and incense shops. At the crossroads with Kwok Man Road, on your right, there is an earth god shrine. Go straight ahead onto Pak She Street. Further along, on the right, the hall of another local association is open to the street. Photos on the wall show Cheung Chau as it was in 1927 and 1953.

Morning walker

Cooling verandahs for colonial policemen

Pak Tai, the god of the north, dominates northern Cheung Chau

The street opens onto the forecourt of the Pak Tai Temple, the island's most famous. It's here that the annual bun festival is held. The temple was built in 1783, following an outbreak of plague on Cheung Chau which was banished when an image of Pak Tai was brought to the island. Amongst the usual drums and bells inside, you'll find an iron sword and a Qing-dynasty sedan chair which are carried on parade with the Pak Tai statue during the bun festival.

Basketball courts extend to the harbour. Turn left onto the praya, which is lined with open-air seafood restaurants. Your cultural expedition should end with a good meal, and this is the perfect place for it. The ferry pier is just a five-minute walk along the waterfront.

Feast before the ferry

Central's freehold oasis: St. John's Cathedral

Churches of Central

2 HOURS

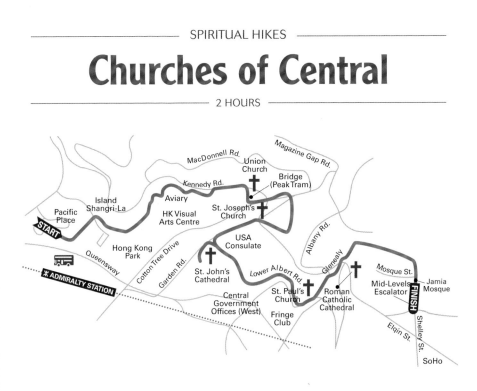

The slopes above Central were settled early on in Hong Kong's development. Besides the mansions of merchants and officials, churches, schools and clubs quickly populated the hillsides leading up to the Peak. Although some of the original buildings are long gone, many of these institutions remain in place in slightly newer premises.

From Pacific Place, take the escalator which travels up to Hong Kong Park. On entry, check the mapboard and make your way to the Visual Arts Centre. It's on the park's far side, so on the way over, take time to check out the aviary and the many water features. The marriage registry is usually busy week-round, as the park's landscaped surroundings are a favourite location for wedding photos.

Wedding in the park

Beautiful botany in the heart of the business district

Vividly hued visitor

Exotic aviary resident

Colonial-era Cassels Block

The Visual Arts Centre is housed in the colonnaded Cassels Block, which was built in the early 1900s as army married quarters (Hong Kong Park was originally the site of Victoria Barracks). It's been cleverly adapted for modern use as an exhibition venue. Take the steps up beside the building to its main entrance, and then step onto Kennedy Road.

Opposite, no. 28 is a handsome mansion. Dating from the same period as Cassels Block, it has been put to use as a bank, a school and a residents' club. In the 1990s it served as offices for the Joint Liaison Group, the body tasked with finalizing arrangements for Hong Kong's handover. Now it's the Hong Kong Design Centre. It's often open to the public. To its right, the buildings of St. Paul's Co-educational College stretch uphill to Macdonnell Road. The institution was founded in 1915, and became the first school in Hong Kong to educate boys and girls together. These buildings date from 1927.

The Peak Tram glides overhead

Further along, the interdenominational Union Church was founded in 1890, according to its foundation stone, but the current buildings date from 1954. Facing it stands Zetland Hall, the discreet location of Hong Kong's Masonic Temple. The Freemasons have met here on Kennedy Road since 1949, after their original lodge on Ice House Street suffered wartime damage.

The bridge over the road here carries the rails of the Peak Tram. Pass through the rainbow-painted archway and turn right, and you'll come to the well-hidden Kennedy Road station of the tramway, 184 feet above sea level. Not many people use these intermediate stops. There is only one tram going up and down all day, and you should be able to see it go by if you wait for a few minutes.

Backtrack and follow the steps down. They lead you underneath Cotton Tree Drive and into the

Union Church on Kennedy Road

compound of St. Joseph's Church. There has been a Catholic church on this site since 1872, but the original building was destroyed by a typhoon. The current one dates from 1968, and it shows. There is a grotto to the Virgin Mary in the grounds, surrounded by candles.

Following the blue railings to the right of the church takes you above the back yard of the Helena May, the entrance to which is on Garden Road. It's an imposing building which was opened in 1916 as a residence and club for women, and it has retained that purpose to the present day. Its airy dining room is a very pleasant old-world place to enjoy lunch.

Carry on downhill, but as you pass the Helena May, turn and look back to your right to see the twin bell towers of St. Joseph's College. Painted in attractive blue and white, this edifice was built in the 1920s. Cross busy

Modernist style of Catholic St. Joseph's

The Helena May: home to expat women since 1916

St. Joseph's College occupies the former Club Germania buildings

Garden Road here and carry on downhill on the other side, crossing Lower Albert Road. Just after the bus stop, black-and-yellow gates open into the compound of St. John's Cathedral, the city's oldest church. (If the gates are closed, then the entry way further down is always open). Built in 1849, it stands on the only parcel of freehold land in Hong Kong – all other land is held on lease from the government.

The Anglican cathedral is built in Gothic style, and the congregation adapted to the tropical climate by introducing swaying punkas, an Anglo-Indian invention, to help air circulate. It suffered extensive damage during the Second World War, including the loss of all its original stained glass windows. Major rebuilding was carried out following the conflict. The current bells were presented to the cathedral on the occasion of Queen Elizabeth's coronation in 1953.

Choir service in the Gothic environs of St. John's Cathedral

The surroundings are leafy and peaceful, despite being just yards away from both Garden Road and Queen's Road Central. On the far side of the compound, the attractive red-brick building is Hong Kong's Court of Final Appeal, housed in what used to be the French Mission. A crest on the south wall marked M. E. (for Missions Etrangères) is from 1917, but the building had many owners before then, and probably dates from the mid-1800s.

Return to Garden Road and turn right, then right again onto Lower Albert Road. You soon arrive at the gates of the Central Government Offices, which will look familiar if you have ever watched a protest on the television news. It is these 1950s buildings which will become redundant if the new government headquarters are built at Tamar. The high fences around them were added only after the handover.

Just after you pass the Hong Kong Central Hospital, the Bishop's House appears up on your left. This was built in 1848 as a seminary to train

The former French Mission

Octagonal tower at Bishop's House

Chinese priests, and also served as the home of St. Paul's College until that school found its own premises. It has an interesting octagonal tower. Opposite, the old Dairy Farm ice house buildings are occupied by the Fringe Club and Foreign Correspondents' Club. Ice was once made here for colonial gin-and-tonics. Both clubs hold exhibitions and events, and the Fringe Club has a rare alfresco spot for drinks on its roof terrace.

Keeping to the left and continuing up Glenealy, you pass St. Paul's Church and its vicarage on your left. Further uphill, at the impressive retaining walls, cross the road and pass the public conveniences to enter the underpass ahead.

Coming out at the far end beside the Zoological & Botanical Gardens, walk ahead a little way and bear right to find the Catholic Cathedral of the Immaculate Conception, completely encircled by taller Caritas buildings and residential towers. Built in 1888 to replace an earlier structure the cathedral

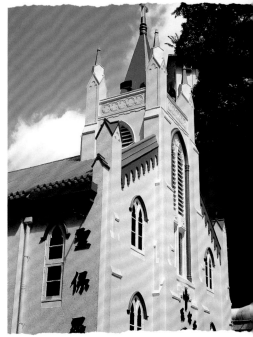

The icehouse: now an entertainment venue   *St. Paul's Church*

Cathedral of the Immaculate Conception, hidden away behind Caine Road

occupied on Wellington Street, it owes its founding largely to the efforts of Italian missionary societies and of Theodore Joset, a Swiss priest. Joset trod carefully to avoid upsetting the Portuguese religious establishment in Macau, which had always overseen Catholic affairs on the China coast – but when he finally revealed his decree from Rome,

Priests in procession

removing Hong Kong from Macau's jurisdiction, there was outrage and he was told to leave the Portuguese colony within 24 hours.

The cathedral's Italian connections helped it avoid the serious looting suffered by other churches during the Second World War, since Italy was allied with Japan.

From the entrance to the compound, a set of steps lead uphill. Take them to the top, and turn right onto Robinson Road, continuing straight ahead onto Mosque Street to meet the Mid-Levels Escalator. Turning right brings you to the wrought-iron gate of the Jamia Mosque, built in 1915 by Essack Elias, a native of Bombay. It originally catered to the Muslim Indians who manned the police force and prison service. You're welcome to enter the shaded and peaceful grounds. A line of surviving houses facing the mosque's front porch represent the real old Hong Kong – once typical of the Mid-Levels, they are now more reminiscent of the back streets of Macau.

Following the escalator down Shelley Street brings you quickly to the SoHo district, where you can rest your legs and quench your thirst at any of a wide choice of bars and cafés.

Mid-Levels minaret

Shek Pik: a panoramic prospect for a picnic

FormAsia thanks you for choosing this guidebook. Our thirty years of publishing experience in Hong Kong means we are unabashed to say that it is the best of its kind, and its text, photography and maps will hopefully set you on a journey of discovery which will enlighten and intrigue. We encourage you to continue this journey by exploring other titles in our diverse range: meticulously created books which offer fascinating insights and curiosities into the art, architecture, history, handicrafts and culture of Asia. This great continent is our home, and we want you to appreciate it as much as we do.

Skylines: *Hong Kong*

Hong Kong's skyline is ever in transition, a flamboyant affirmation of this city's determination to let nothing stand in its way as it forges full steam ahead into the future. This volume serves both as tribute to the restless spirit of a city forever creating better and grander manifestations of itself, and as a reminder of whence it came, as enshrined in the few traces of antiquity that survive that headlong progress.

Building Hong Kong

Its Architecture is Hong Kong's sublime art, conditioning the way this ever-changing city has evolved. The thrust is more upward than outward, shaping the vertical profile of this intensely concentrated metropolis and ensuring that, whatever changes are in store, Hong Kong continues building its fabled reputation as the '*Many Splendoured Thing*'.

Passing Shadows

The photographers who compiled a detailed record of a bygone Hong Kong have handed down to us a rich inheritance. Their Passing Shadows leave an imprint on these pages so palpable one can almost reach out and touch the long demolished stones of that vanished metropolis, populated by a people we never met and pursuing a lifestyle far removed from Hong Kong of today.

Hong Kong: What's In – What's Out

Takes you to the heart and soul of one of the world's most fabulous cities. Discover where to go, what you should know, where to sleep, what to eat; What's in; what's out. What's indoors; what's outdoors. What's fashionable; what isn't. What's hot; what's not. What to do; what not to do . . . All of these, and much more, are packed into this most comprehensive, up-to-the-minute guide ever published on Hong Kong.

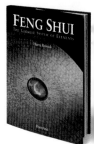

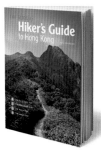

The Serious Hiker's Guide

High ridges, sparkling waterfalls, lush feng shui woods and ancient fishing communities nestled in rocky harbours. The Hiker's Guide will direct your course into that other Hong Kong which lies outside the city margins, easing your transition into a wealth of natural beauty accessible to those ready to venture beyond busy streets and shopping malls.

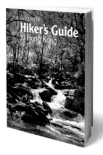

The Leisurely Hiker's Guide

By any measure, Hong Kong is an impressive city. But there is a world beyond the impatient traffic and chic shopping malls: an older place of soot-blackened temples, traditional street markets and colonial-era museums. Travel twenty minutes out of the metropolis, and you'll find stone-laid trails, sheltered beaches and waterfront restaurants galore. The 40-guided walks in this book are quickly reached from public transport, and can be completed in an afternoon – leaving ample time for a leisurely hike to be followed by leisurely dinner.

Feng Shui

As elusive in its explanation as the power of prophecy, feng shui is the spiritual magnetic field that binds our universe, distinguishing good from ill, peace from turmoil, governing the balance in the very elements of harmony itself. Understanding it is beyond the capacity of most laymen. Not crediting it is like not believing in the inevitability of spring replacing winter.

Buddha: *In Life and Art*

No memorials throughout history have towered higher than the many monuments to Buddha scattered across Asia. The serene form and countenance of these gentle giants represents the attainment of all we seek to be. We stand in awe of their massive passivity, and we wonder at the hands that fashioned wood, stone and metal into such sublime grace.

Chinese Symbolism:
The sublime language

Pictograms, through which earliest mankind endeavoured to communicate, achieved their richest profusion in China, and gave rise to the world's most complex – and, many would argue, most artistic – written language. This book surveys some of the best recognised examples – not least of which are the dozen animal signs that comprise the twelve-year cycle of the Chinese zodiac.

Bamboo

Ever the poet's brush, the musician's flute, bamboo has sounded its quiet sonatas through the lives of Asians over countless millennia. From chopsticks to tools of trade, it has fed, housed and furnished their existence, stimulated their intellect and expressed their emotions from the cradle to the grave. Little wonder that many still revere this versatile and tenaciously enduring plant.

The Chinese Scholar's Desk

To the Chinese scholar, the preparation for recording his thought was as important as the execution. On his desk lay the *Four Treasures*, the symbols of his calling: paper, brushes, inkslab and ink, so arranged as to inspire the best of his talent. Calligraphy in China ranked on a par with painting and poetry, as hallmarks of a man of accomplishment and discriminating taste. This book takes the reader into the scholar's study and seats him at that desk.

Chinese Proverbs

Confucius has become the oft-quoted fount of aphorisms and analects far wider and more comprehensive in their didactic scope than any attributed to sages elsewhere in the world. But the real gems of Chinese wisdom lie in the anonymous and ageless proverbs, of which this volume contains a formidable and beautifully illustrated selection. Accompanying the Romanized Chinese version and English translations in this edition are corresponding Chinese calligraphic characters.

Old Hong Kong: *Presentation Edition.*

Three volumes trace the story of Hong Kong from an age of Empire to its return to Chinese sovereignty in 1997. A valuable collection of historic photographs details this chronology of Hong Kong, which for 156 years, flew a foreign flag on the doorstep of China. This extraordinary account is set against the backdrop of the demise of China's last dynasty; the birth of the People's Republic; the rising power of Japan and finally Hong Kong's resurgence in the twilight of the British Empire.

Old Hong Kong:
1860–30 June 1997. Condensed Edition

This remarkable documentation of Hong Kong's colonial history with archival photographs from the world's great libraries, museums and private collections is a condensed edition of FormAsia's award-winning series Old Hong Kong: Volumes I, II & III.
This volume traces the story of Hong Kong from 1860, to its return to Chinese sovereignty on a rain-drenched midnight, 30 June 1997.

CHINA: *A Century of Conflict*

To understand the roaring economic superpower of our age, one has to appreciate the history of one of the world's longest and most enduring cultures. From the opulence of Empire, China declined into continual warfare, humiliation and military defeat – and then confronted the radical change of regime on 1st October 1949.
The dramatic events are documented in this unique book in words and historic black and white photographs, many of which have never been seen publicly before.

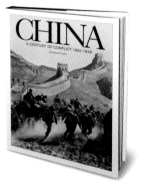

Chinnery in China

George Chinnery was that providential combination of the right man in the right place at the right time. But for him our vision of China in the early 19th century would remain deficient. His was the faithful record of Macau not only in the great panoramas in his oils and watercolours but also of lovingly captured details in his pencil sketches. This book presents a portrait of an old and crotchety but immensely gifted man; just the way Chinnery would have wanted it.

Shek Pik

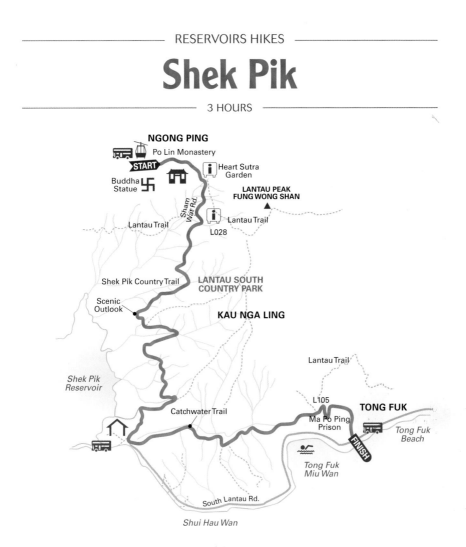

Lantau Peak is ringed by many tracks far less visited than the Lantau Trail. This quiet downhill route winds around its slopes, high above the Shek Pik Reservoir. It is absolutely one of the most pristine hikes in all of Hong Kong. Here one treads on real soil, over granite pavings, traversing genuine stone-laid paths. Please don't tell anyone and certainly not the Leisure and Cultural Services Department, lest it come and cement the entire route to add to its endless umbilical cords of concrete, as if bent on reminding us we can never sever our links with the concrete jungle.

Leaving the Lantau Trail

Take any bus from Mui Wo or Tung Chung up to Po Lin, site of the Big Buddha, and follow the signs to the tea gardens. The route is well marked. After you pass the somewhat dilapidated teahouses, make a right turn over a metal bridge. This puts you on the track for Lantau Peak.

Very soon, you'll reach an open area with map boards and an ornamental gateway. To your right lies the recently opened Heart Sutra Garden. Wooden cabers have been erected in an infinity-style figure of eight, each bearing a verse from the heart sutra, an important Buddhist text. This is probably the most spiritual corner of the entire Ngong Ping Buddhist complex, testifying to the long history of the Ngong Ping Plateau as a place of retreat.

Sutra verses, mountain slopes

The pleasure of old stone paths

Staying put with the contour trail

Looking out past Shek Pik to the Soko Islands

Heading south – bidding the Buddha farewell

Find the yellow sign pointing down to Sham Wat Road. This is your way ahead. It's a narrow, stony path reminiscent of a pony trail.

Take care to leave the Lantau Trail by continuing left at the next fork, towards the Shek Pik catchwater. The Lantau L028 marker is clearly visible here. The track makes a gentle descent southwards, occasionally leaving the open hillside to cross steep seasonal streams.

A glance over your right shoulder, between the shrubbery, will provide a view of the Great Buddha seated serenely on its pedestal, commanding the horizon against the deep blue sky.

Some way down the path, a prominent rocky outcrop provides the perfect place to stop for a snack and a scenic outlook over the broad expanse of water.

The rush of fresh streams after autumn rains

Cascading catchwater

Level catchment trails run the length of Lantau

The reservoir was completed in 1963, and was at that point the largest in Hong Kong. The scheme involved submerging the old Shek Pik village. During excavations, a treasure trove of ancient coins and pottery was discovered, dating back to the Sung dynasty. It was speculated that this may have belonged to the court of the two boy emperors who spent some time on Lantau while fleeing the Mongols.

Out to sea, the uninhabited Soko Islands on the horizon straddle the route to Macau. Here one can sit and watch the jetfoils zip by.

Soon the path starts to descend more steeply down man-made concrete steps, where woodland obscures your view. Crossing a bridge, you reach the level catchwater trail which runs almost the entire length of Lantau Island. It's this channel which is used to fill the reservoir.

If you're in a hurry, you can bear right here and walk ahead to the South Lantau Road. Otherwise, turn left and follow the catchwater for a while. This section of the catchment is stepped. After rainfall, the sound of cascading water is a beautiful addition to your surroundings.

The trail follows the contour of the hillside, passing tributaries and barbecue areas. One path branches off downhill to Shui Hau. Don't take this turn-off but pass it and carry on until the road forks. On the corner you'll find the Lantau L105 marker and a yellow sign pointing to Tung Chung, 3 kms and 3/4 hour away. A bench has been provided at this corner. Take the right-hand turning, down past Ma Po Ping detention centre, to reach Tong Fuk village which lies 100 metres to the left.

From here, buses run back to Tung Chung or Mui Wo, and you can enjoy a cold beer with boerewors (farmer's sausage) while you wait at the South African-run Gallery, tel: 2980-2582. The buses stop directly in front of the restaurant. Or, if you still have time, you could cross the road, follow the path across the field, and search for hermit crabs on the village beach.

汝南世澤

鐵笛家聲

Door god stands guard at the Pai Tau village temple

Ten Thousand Buddhas Monastery

1 HOUR

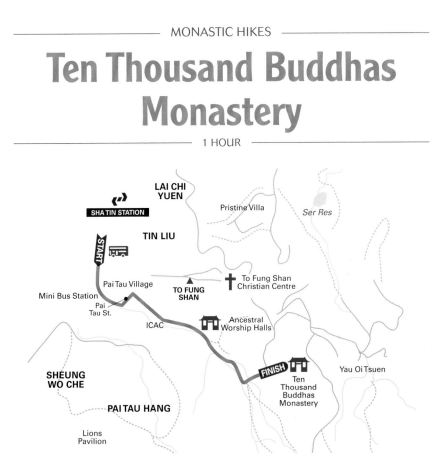

The teeming new town of Sha Tin no longer boasts the sandy fields its name represents. But some of its former rural character lies unchanged, on the less frenetic side of the railway line.

Take the KCR from Hung Hom or Kowloon Tong to Sha Tin station. Instead of joining the river of humanity flowing towards New Town Plaza, take the northern exit for the green minibus terminus. Turn left and descend by way of the slope to Pai Tau Village.

The quieter side of Sha Tin

This way to enlightenment

The route to the monastery lies uphill, so you are advised to buy drinks in one of the village shops. Dogs doze in the shade and children play catch. One gets the feeling that little has changed here since steam trains chugged past on their way to the border.

Head in the general direction of Pai Tak Street and at Pai Tau Street bear left. Immediately before the imposing Shatin District Office complex turn right into Sheung Wo Che Road, walking past the ICAC office entrances, and turn left at the clearly visible sign of 10,000 Buddhas. Avoid the pagoda-like structure with covered escalators leading to it on the hill behind the Shatin District Office, as that is an ancestor memorial.

Fibreglass monks line the route

The signposted path leads up the valley rising gradually as it passes village houses, overgrown farm buildings and former pig sheds. Although most traces of agriculture have disappeared, a bee farm remains and visitors can buy honey.

The steps become steeper, and a parade of golden fibreglass statues heralds your arrival at the path leading to the Ten Thousand Buddhas Monastery. There are in fact around 13,000 tiny Buddhas lining the walls of the main hall; the term 'ten thousand' is a Chinese phrase which can otherwise be translated as 'myriad'. In addition to the Buddhas, there is some gaudy outdoor statuary and a nine-storey pagoda.

The founder of the monastery, abbot Yuet Kai, died in 1965, just eight years after the complex was completed. His corpse was exhumed eight months later and found to be intact – at least relatively – and so his followers had his body gilded. It rests in a glass case.

Here the Bodhisattvas come in all sizes, shapes and attitudes

Benign representations of the Sage

Pagodas and statues within an air of calm and repose

If the sight of a golden cadaver does not put you off, you can enjoy a good and cheap vegetarian lunch at the monastery's simple dining hall.

Other temples are located a little higher up the hillside; there is even a ruined pavilion beside a secluded waterfall, presenting a very peaceful scene. A separate stairway leads back downhill to the KCR.

A corner of a foreign field is forever Trappist

Trappist Monastery

2 HOURS

Trappist Dairy milk bottles are a familiar sight in any convenience store in town. The cattle have nowadays moved to greener pastures; but the Trappist monastery still stands high on the coast of Lantau Island, overlooking the Western Harbour.

Take the ferry from Pier 3 in Central to Discovery Bay. Turn left upon arrival and walk past the bus station, over the slight hill and down to the sandy bay of Nim Shue Wan. This seaside village existed long before Discovery Bay was conceived; and now many of its houses are home to domestic helpers who work in the new development.

The trail leads southwards along the coast, passing an ancient and very stationary Land Rover which was apparently once used by the Trappist monks to transport fresh milk. The path opens out onto a wider track. The fourth Station of the Cross is marked on a tree opposite. Turn right and walk uphill to reach the monastery buildings – a signpost which originally pointed in this direction has been largely consumed by white ants.

Free-range cattle roam the Lantau peaks

50,000 miles, single owner

Into the bush in a spiritual frame of mind

If in a spiritual frame of mind, you could choose to turn left here instead, and descend a short distance to the monks' jetty – from where you can backtrack and follow all 14 stages of Christ's suffering uphill, from the seashore to the monastery.

Long since banished from Beijing

An alternative route to this point is to take the ferry from Central to Peng Chau, and then transfer to the wooden 'kaido' or village ferry which runs to an irregular schedule. This ancient vessel will deposit you either at Nim Shue Wan, from where you can follow the same path as above; or at the Tai Shui Hang jetty, from which point you can follow the wider track uphill.

This order of Trappist monks originally had their base in Beijing, but were dispersed after the 1949 communist victory and eventually settled here on Lantau. The monks take a vow of silence, and passers-by are asked to speak in quiet tones.

As you ascend the incline, you pass a number of well-kept old buildings surrounded by lush greenery. A bridge leads over a steep river to a particularly appealing group of chapels and quarters. Above these stands a shed of antique farm machinery, cloaked in a general air of benign neglect. Take the narrower path ahead here, beside the stream. It leads gradually uphill, winding around the back of the monastery grounds, until the brush falls away and you find yourself scaling open hillside.

Crossing the bridge, crossing the stream

Chapels of quietude

A brisk climb brings you up to a viewing pavilion, where a magnificent panorama opens up at your feet, encompassing much of Lantau, most of the outlying isles and large parts of Kowloon, the New Territories and Hong Kong Island. The ferry pier at Silvermine Bay – this hike's final destination – lies below you to the south.

Discovery Bay jet-ferry returns to Central

The descent from here is a simple matter of sticking to the track as it aims towards the well-used beach at Tung Wan Tau. Follow the coastal path around to the town, and enjoy dinner or drinks before boarding the ferry back to Central.

Central walkways

30 MINUTES

With the opening of the new Star Ferry pier and its attached walkway, it's sobering to think that one can now walk from the middle of Victoria Harbour all the way to Conduit Road in the Mid-Levels without one's feet touching the ground. Many indoor sections feature the comfort – or discomfort, depending on your mode of dress – of icy air-conditioning, but all offer shelter from the torrential rains of summer. This walk describes a few of the places which can be reached by a combination of overhead walkways, shopping malls and escalators.

ifc: impregnable fortress of consumerism

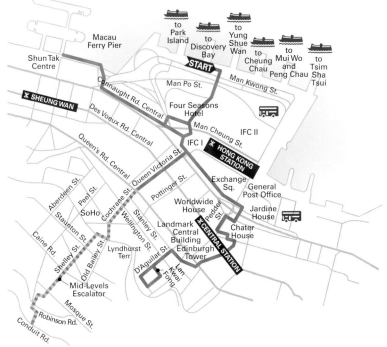

Water transport awaits

From the Outlying Island ferry piers in Central, take the escalator which travels up between Piers 3 and 4. There's an outdoor café on the roof of the Discovery Bay pier which is good for harbourfront drinks at night. Follow the walkway over an empty green space to enter IFC Mall, where the City'super food hall and the Palace IFC arthouse cinema feed the body and mind respectively. It's a posh mall, with passages leading to the Lane Crawford department store and the Four Seasons Hotel; the attached office tower soars to a vertigo-inducing 88 storeys above the harbour.

Aiming straight ahead and bearing right, you enter the circular core of One IFC. Take the glass doors on the far side and turn immediately left onto the elevated walkway. Here you're walking alongside the podium of Exchange Square, home to the stock exchange and the offices of myriad banks. Until the mid-1990s round of reclamation which gave us the IFC and the Airport Express station, this podium overlooked the waterfront and the old ferry piers.

Approaching Jardine House, that building of a thousand portholes, turn right to cross over Connaught Road. You're led into Worldwide House, a warren of remittance centres and

Portholes reflected in Chater House

Imported foodstuffs   *Glad rags galore*   *Shoppers come and go*

shops stocking imported Philippine products. This occupies the site of the colonial-era General Post Office, which was demolished in the 1970s during the construction of the first MTR line. Turn left to exit the building and cross via walkway into the haute couture environs of Chater House. Sir Catchick Paul Chater was an Armenian from Calcutta who arrived in Hong Kong at the age of 18, and quickly made his fortune. He co-founded the Hong Kong Land company, and was responsible for much of the early reclamation of Central and Kowloon.

Stock exchange sculptures: moving toward a bull market?

The Landmark: for ladies who lunch

Floral fashion

A watch fit for a starlet

Turn right again to enter Alexandra House, carrying on straight ahead into The Landmark. On your way across Des Voeux Road Central, you have a classic view of masses of pedestrians battling buses and trams at the junction of Pedder Street: a scene which is televised nightly to illustrate just about any news story going. The road is named for Sir George William Des Voeux, governor from 1887 to 1891, who arrived in Hong Kong at the end of his career in the foreign service. Hong Kong was slower in pace then. "A governor might pass the whole of his tenure of office by doing little more than sign his name to the productions of others," Des Voeux happily remarked. "The place would be a paradise to a man inclined to be idle."

He might have included women in his statement. The Landmark's atrium café is, after all, a favourite haunt of tea-sipping tai-tais. Head for the far right-hand corner of the mall, where a spiral staircase winds its way above HMV into an upper level of the Central Building: a tiny pampered oasis of ladies' spas and beauty counters. Here you cross Queen's Road to enter the first-floor marble lobby of Central Tower, which was graced for a while by stands of bamboo until it became apparent they couldn't long survive the glacial indoor conditions.

Beauty for sale

Rub-down relaxation

Fiesta in the Fong *Cash flow, contraflow*

Make a right turn to follow another walkway into the Entertainment Building – an office tower which isn't particularly amusing, but perhaps derives its name from the King's Theatre which long stood on this Queen's Road plot. A staircase leads down to D'Aguilar Street, upon which you can turn left and fight your way through a mad crush of taxis up to Lan Kwai Fong. Watch out also for packs of office workers who must throng the streets en masse at lunchtimes due to inflexible working practices.

Central has other walkways too. Going straight ahead from One IFC, you pass through the first floor level of the modern Hang Seng Bank Building. The bank was founded in 1933 as a Dickensian abacus-and-scrolls operation, but the name chosen ("Ever Growing") proved fortuitous: now it is one of the biggest banks in town, and the Hong Kong stock exchange index carries its moniker. The route carries on through the condemned Bauhaus-style Central Market to reach the start of the Mid-Levels Escalator, which travels uphill past the bars and cafés of SoHo to the Jamia Mosque on Shelley Street, ending on Conduit Road.

Turning right from IFC sets you on an overhead route past office buildings to the Shun Tak Centre, named for the Pearl River Delta home town of its builder, casino magnate Stanley Ho. A waterfront section of walkway allows you to watch gambler-laden jetfoils and helicopters noisily setting off for Macau. The walkway exits the far side of the Shun Tak Centre to descend to street level beside the Edwardian edifice of Western Market.

The ups and downs of office life

Rapid getaway to Macau

Autumn waters plunge into Bride's Pool

Plover Cove and Bride's Pool

4 HOURS

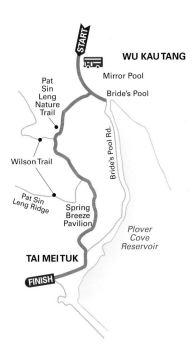

Hong Kong's water shortages were so acute in the 1960s that innovative solutions were required – what would today be termed 'blue-sky thinking'. The major problem was that no land could be spared to build new reservoirs. An audacious scheme was hatched: engineers would block off a sea inlet with a giant dam, pump out the trapped seawater, and fill it with fresh water from a far-flung network of hillside conduits. The plan succeeded, and Plover Cove became the world's first 'reservoir-in-the-sea'. This hike takes you on a route high along its western edge.

Old stone bridges still link villages

Spring water follows a stony course

Take the KCR to Tai Po Market, and follow the underpass into the bus station below Uptown Plaza. If it's a Sunday, you can take bus 275R to its terminus on Bride's Pool Road. On weekdays, there's a green minibus (no. 20C) but it runs only hourly. You're better off taking an $80 taxi ride. You should alight at the bus terminus on Bride's Pool Road, shortly before the turning to Wu Kau Tang.

Leaving the bus stop, backtrack a little down the road before turning left to join the Bride's Pool Nature Trail. It leads into a cool, shaded valley of woodland streams. The signposted path crosses old village bridges where watercourses meet, and then bears left to reach the locally famous beauty spot of Bride's Pool. Take the stone path uphill in the direction of Chiu Keng Tam to reach the place.

Trail meets road

A waterfall here plunges into the pool. The story goes that a Qing-dynasty bride was being carried by sedan chair to her new husband's home, but one of her bearers lost his footing on the slippery stones. Chair and bride fell into the water far below, and the bride was drowned. It is said that she still views her reflection in nearby Mirror Pool while brushing her hair.

Descending once more but bearing right the path reaches the road again. You must cross over now to join the Pat Sin Leng Nature Trail. This section of the trail leads straight uphill, and before long you're treated to views in various directions: the Wu Kau Tang villages below, the vast reservoir to the east, Shenzhen far to the north, and all the open hill country in between.

Forest stream, cool and shaded

Woodland waters flow freely

The freshwater reservoir fills the former cove

Plover Cove is named not for the bird but after the Royal Navy ship which originally surveyed these shores in the 1840s. Several old Hakka villages were submerged when the reservoir was finally filled. Once upon a time, the inhabitants worked the pearl-laden oyster beds of these deep waters – a dangerous but lucrative trade.

The Wilson Trail joins the track from the right, and stays with the nature trail across the next few steep stream valleys before it departs to strike steeply uphill. You should keep left. The path begins a gentle descent from this point, looking south across Tolo Harbour all the way to Ma On Shan.

After passing the Spring Breeze Pavilion – which commemorates the members of a school party who died in a hill fire in 1996 – you reach a country parks visitor centre which has an exhibition of local culture, flora and fauna. From here, follow the road downhill a short distance to Tai Mei Tuk. The village is a popular place for barbecues: a large waterfront barbecue site is found on the far side of the bus rank. Follow the road along the shore from here, past the youth hostel and sailing centres, to reach the main dam of the Plover Cove Reservoir.

Spring Breeze Pavilion

At 2km in length, it is Hong Kong's longest dam, and it rises as high as a nine-storey building. Such huge bulk is a necessity – it holds back the weight of 230 million cubic metres of water. The exposed dam is a good place to fly kites.

On the way back to Tai Mei Tuk, you are looking straight up at Pat Sin Leng – the ridge of towering peaks named after the eight immortals of Chinese legend. Besides barbecue sites, the village has a line of busy restaurants which will be pleased to welcome you before you catch the 75K bus back to Tai Po.

Opposite Ma On Shan, the 2km-long dam supports the weight of over 200 million cubic litres of water

Ancient interior of the temple to two deities

Man Mo Temple

1 HOUR

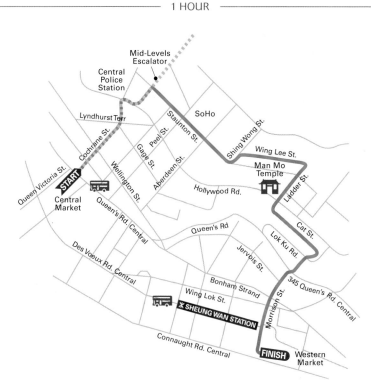

Hollywood Road's Man Mo Temple is one of the best known in Hong Kong. As its name ('Literary and Military') suggests, it is dedicated to two separate gods who represent culture and soldiery respectively. This walk takes you on a brief tour of the surrounding old sections of Central and Sheung Wan.

Take the Star Ferry, MTR or tram to Central, and head for the old Central Market on Des Voeux Road and Queen Victoria Street. This Bauhaus-style building, erected in 1939, is one of Central's oldest but is currently threatened with demolition. The fish and vegetable traders were kicked out a few years ago. Take the escalator up to its mezzanine level and turn left.

Commuting by escalator

Walking ahead, you quickly join the celebrated Mid-Levels Escalator, an open-air travelator system that carries commuters to and from their offices without the need for buses or taxis. Local tourism officials boast of it being 'the world's longest outdoor escalator,' but their claim is challenged by more sceptical residents, who contend that it is "just a lot of short escalators joined together". Still, there's no doubt that its construction has rejuvenated the older areas of Central which line its route. As you ascend the hill in the stately manner it allows, you'll pass health stores, coffee shops, boutiques, yoga centres and spas, few of which existed ten years ago.

The 1919 façade of the old Central Police Station

Local character: commercial streets feature scores of signboards

The escalator turns right as it crosses Hollywood Road – giving you a view of the Victorian-era Central Police Station compound on your left – and then straightens itself out again to enter Mid-Levels proper. Stepping onto Staunton Street, you're firmly in the upscale dining area now known as SoHo. Chic international restaurants beckon from every shopfront, often changing names, cuisines, chefs and owners every few months. Turn right and walk the gauntlet of these hip eateries.

Parts of the neighbourhood still retain their former flavour – the octogenarian lantern maker made decorations for the Coronation in 1953 and is still in business – and you'll catch a whiff of timeless incense as you pass the shrine on Peel Street nearby.

Things quieten down a little as you step, across Elgin and then Aberdeen Streets, onto Bridges Street. As you approach the small market building, take a left uphill onto Shing Wong Street, and then the first right. Wing Lee Street is a line of traditional Hong Kong tenements which have survived from another era. Several still have antique printing presses operating from their ground floors. Carry on through the small garden with its tall shady trees to Ladder Street at the far end.

Soho's lantern artisan

Peel Street shrine

Man Mo temple

Quiet back lanes of Central

This area of stone stairways is a good indication of what the Mid-Levels were like before the advent of the motor car. The district ahead of you was formerly known as Tai Ping Shan, and in the 19th century was a hotbed of crime, disease and prostitution. Finally, an outbreak of the plague prompted the authorities to raze the whole area, paving the way for many subsequent renovations that have led to the present configuration.

Follow the steps downhill to Hollywood Road. Despite Hong Kong's high-profile film industry, the street's name refers to the Irish estate of a former governor, rather than any links to Tinseltown.

The Man Mo Temple is on your right. It's well accustomed to tourists, so don't be timid: enter and have a look around. It's usually awash in a blue haze from the smoke of the coiled incense hanging from the ceiling. It was allegedly built by Cheung Po Tsai, the doyen of Hong Kong pirates.

Take the steps downhill on the other side of the road. These lead you onto Upper Lascar Row or, as it is better known, 'Cat Street'. It's a collection of antique shops, second-hand stores and bric-a-brac stalls. In former times, it was a thieves' market – and it was said that if something was stolen from you in the morning, you could find it here by the evening. Today, it's a good place for souvenirs.

Any of the alleyways on your right will lead you down to Queen's Road Central, and you should then find Morrison Street beside the giant municipal services building. Follow it down towards the harbour. The handsome edifice of Western Market appears shortly on your left, partly hidden by an MTR cooling tower. This Edwardian building has recently been renovated and houses small shops, including a Chinese dessert house. Enjoy a cool concoction of mango or ginger before boarding a tram back to Central.

Soldier on and you may find a bargain

Pre and post revolutionary bric-a-brac on Cat Street

Edwardian roof space houses a dim sum restaurant

Western Market faces the harbour

Line of sight: keep an eye out for the tram

Hong Kong Racing Museum and Queen's Road East

1.5 HOURS

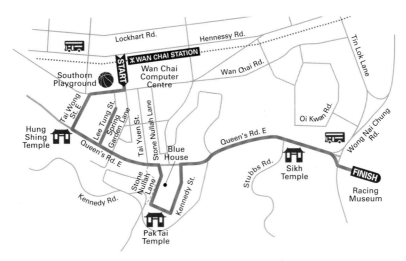

Horse races have been held at Happy Valley for at least 160 years, and the gambling monopoly held by the Jockey Club has generated billions of dollars for local charities and community projects. The Club has opened a museum beside the racecourse which tells the story of Hong Kong racing. This walk also includes many antiquities around Queen's Road East.

Leave Wan Chai MTR station by Exit B2 and turn immediately left to reach Johnston Road. Turn right to skirt the football pitch at Southorn Playground, and cross the tram line towards the old buildings on the opposite corner. These shophouses are characteristic of old Hong Kong, and although their plot is being redeveloped, the facades will remain.

Silver steed

The pitched roof old Post Office

Keeping them on your right, follow Tai Wong Street East until you reach the main road. Cross over to enter the Hung Shing temple.

The temple was built in the mid-1800s and was then close to the shoreline. It was built around seashore boulders which are still in place. If you go inside, you'll see that much of the interior is occupied by a large outcrop of rock. It's an untidy, soot-blackened space which feels rather ancient. Besides Hung Shing, there are altars to other gods like Kwun Yam and Kam Fa, and a little cherub figure suspended from the rafters. Outside the temple there is a furnace – the temple keeper puts worshippers' joss sticks in there when the altar bowls get too crowded.

Cockatoo – crested visitor to Wan Chai's trees

Leaving the temple, turn right to continue down Queen's Road East. On the opposite side of the road there is another terrace of traditional shophouses, but crosses on their windows signal their approaching disappearance. The next turning on the left is Lee Tung Street – better known as Wedding Card Street – a collection of typical 1950s buildings famous as a place to get invitation cards printed. Red protest banners hang from signboards; the entire street is to be demolished by the Urban Renewal Authority, dispersing a long-established community and forcing most of the wedding card printers to cease business. The silver lining to this cloud is that an anti-redevelopment campaign drew wide support, perhaps marking a turning point in public appreciation of Hong Kong's remaining heritage.

Till death us do part: Wedding Card Street has closed its doors

Redundant signboards of Lee Tung Street

Back-street balconies: the Blue House

Carrying on, you soon reach the tiny old Wanchai Post Office, which dates from 1913. Shaded by a mango tree, the pitched-roof building is now used as an Environmental Resource Centre. A little further on, the old Wanchai Market comes into view. Built in the Bauhaus style in 1937, it's an elegant structure which is also to be demolished by myopic town planners.

Before you reach the market, turn right into Stone Nullah Lane. An old blue house here still possesses wrought-iron balconies, which were once a common sight above city streets. It also has old-style wooden staircases, and no flushing water – nightsoil collectors still visit the building. Note the large windows on all sides: a legacy of the days before air-conditioning, when air flow was more important. The yellow buildings around the corner on Hing Wan Street are also lovely examples of local architecture from the 1920s.

At the top of Stone Nullah Lane you'll find the large Pak Tai temple, the grounds of which have recently been renovated in an attractive Japanese style. The building is beautifully kept. It dates from the same period as the Hung Shing temple, although the bronze statue inside was cast much earlier, in 1604.

Aged banyan in the Pak Tai courtyard

Leaving the temple, which is open from 8:00am-5:00pm daily, turn right and take the steps down to Kennedy Street, which leads past motor repair shops and the Street Sleeper's Association and back to Queen's Road East. Turn right again, crossing Kennedy Road towards Wah Yan College. On either side of the school's driveway there are wartime air-raid tunnels set into the hillside. This part of town saw fierce hand-to-hand fighting between British and Japanese forces in 1941. Further along, you may spot a pair of small granite stones engraved with the Admiralty's anchor emblem – these may have something to do with the former Royal Naval Hospital, which stood on the hill above Wanchai Market until the 1940s.

Granite anchor, a naval marker

Lady's insignia for a post-war racing season

Royal club badge

The Queen Mother's Cup

Access all areas: member's pass

They Sikh him here: Khalsa Diwan

Crossing Stubbs Road, you pass the Sikh Temple (see p.251) and then, further down, the Cosmopolitan Hotel. This was until 1997 the local headquarters of the Xinhua news agency, and thus the de facto embassy of China. Protesters against various central government policies were often camped out in the garden opposite.

To get to the Racing Museum you need to take the tunnel under Wong Nei Chung Road. The museum is on the second floor of the Happy Valley Stand, and is open from 10:00am to 5:00pm every day except Monday.

Admission is free. The museum overlooks the racecourse, and photos recount the history of local racing from the 1840s – when Happy Valley was reclaimed from swampland – to the present day. A central exhibit is the skeleton of a champion steed.

To return to the MTR, turn right upon exiting the museum and make your way north to Times Square.

Stiff upper lips for a sepia-toned racing meet

Flooded valleys in Hong Kong Island's backyard

Tai Tam & Wong Nei Chung

3 HOURS

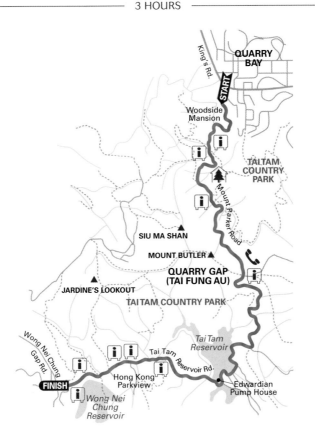

Tai Tam Country Park is a great green lung occupying much of the eastern half of Hong Kong Island. Its high uplands are crossed by both the Hong Kong Trail and Wilson Trail, and within and around its borders can be found five reservoirs created in the first 80 years of Hong Kong's founding as a colony. In fact, it was these water catchments which saved the area from development long enough for it to be incorporated as a country park. This hike departs directly from the city, but delivers you in short order to places green and peaceful.

Take the MTR to Quarry Bay and leave the station by Exit A. Turn right onto King's Road, passing the modern offices at Taikoo Place, and walk ahead until you meet Mount Parker Road coming from the right. It's a single-track road built to allow access to the wireless station on Mount Parker. Leading inland, it starts to climb the hillside, reaching tree cover very quickly.

The first landmark on your right is Woodside, a red-brick mansion built by Swire in 1917 as staff quarters for the Taikoo sugar refinery in Quarry Bay. Taikoo sugar is still on supermarket shelves today, but the refinery has been redeveloped into Taikoo Place. 'Taikoo' is in fact the Chinese name for Swire, who remain the biggest landlord in Quarry Bay with such housing estates as Taikoo Shing ('Swire City'), built on the site of the old dockyard.

Harbour views recede as you climb higher

Further up, the Wilson Trail crosses our route, but we remain on Mount Parker Road. It climbs ever higher, but after about an hour you should reach Quarry Gap ('Great Wind Gap' in Chinese), the highest point of this hike. Until 1929, there was a funicular railway running up to this spot from Quarry Bay, carrying the families of sugar refinery and dockyard workers up to the mountains to enjoy cooler air. After your climb, you probably wish it was still operating.

Red-brick relic: Woodside

From here on, though, it's all downhill. Ahead and below, the secret valleys of Tai Tam are laid open, reflective reservoirs surrounded by a ring of green peaks. You descend through thick forest, eventually turning right at a fork to reach the tiered dam of the Tai Tam Upper Reservoir, built in 1889. Cross it and follow the Hong Kong Trail around to the granite edges of the Tai Tam Byewash Reservoir.

Picnic sites a-plenty

Here, past an Edwardian pumphouse, stands a tall, triangular milestone which is the last of its kind. It was erected in the 1840s, along with many others, to mark the route of the first road between Victoria (as the city was then called) and Stanley. This road followed the coast from modern-day Central to Aberdeen, then passed through

First glimpse of the South

Limpid waters reflect your progress

Wong Nei Chung Gap to Tai Tam, and thence south to Stanley. It bears the Chinese characters 'kwan tai lo', and though there has been much speculation, nobody has yet been able to explain their meaning.

Turn back now and take the first left turn, crossing between the reservoirs. This sets you on a much-walked stretch of Tai Tam Reservoir Road, and it is free of traffic until you reach the residential towers of Parkview. Following the road sharply downhill, you arrive at the Wong Nei Chung Reservoir, built in 1899 and much smaller than its country park neighbours. It has a café, and you can hire pedalos to join the terrapins and ducks out on the water.

Granite spans the valley

Century in stone

Edwardian Pump House

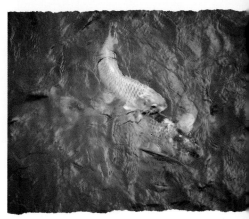

Emblem of harmony: pairs of carp in Wong Nei Chung reservoir

(For a longer but level alternative route to this point from the triangular milestone, you can follow a quiet catchwater trail. Turn left immediately after crossing the reservoir, and follow the track around the southern slopes of Violet Hill. The trail gives you views of Repulse Bay and Deepwater Bay and ends directly at the Wong Nei Chung dam).

To get back to town, buses and taxis can be found further down the hill at Wong Nei Chung Gap Road.

The ornate rooflines of King Yin Li have watched over the city's growth

The Police Museum and the Aberdeen reservoirs

2 HOURS

Taking the bus up to The Peak is a scenic alternative to the Peak Tram. But it's also a good way to get to Wan Chai Gap, a pass in the hills which is the site of the Police Museum. This hike ends in Aberdeen.

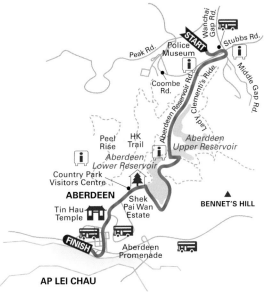

Wan Chai – an alternative angle from Stubbs Road

Take bus 15 from Exchange Square in Central or, on Sundays, bus 15B from Tin Hau MTR. The route travels above Happy Valley and up Stubbs Road, past the beautiful Chinese-styled King Yin Li mansion, offering wonderful views all the way. You should alight at Wan Chai Gap, which is a meeting of seven roads and lanes, including Coombe Road, Peak Road and Black's Link. (Alternatively, you can walk up to this point by following Wan Chai Gap Road from the old post office on Queen's Road East – a steep but well shaded path).

From the bus stop, backtrack a short way to step onto Coombe Road. The Police Museum is housed in an old police station up on the right, with an antique field gun at its entrance. It has three permanent exhibitions – on narcotics, triad societies and the general history of the formerly-Royal Hong Kong Police Force – and one rotating display which covers subjects like police uniforms or the Marine Police. It's open from 9:00am to 5:00pm, except on Tuesdays when it opens at 2:00pm and Mondays when it's closed. Entry is free.

Emblem of the pre-handover police force

Ceremonial pith helmet of the Governor's Police aide-de-camp

Recognition for exceptional bravery

Georgian era detective's badge

Service revolvers loaded with grounds each

Field gun at Wan Chai Gap

Colonial constables: expedition against pirates

Greenery presses down to the water's edge

Placid blue-green waters above Aberdeen

Stone dam of the upper reservoir

Far-off view of marina and boatyards

A silent escape from the madding city

Upon leaving, cross Coombe Road to the public garden. You need to find the start of the pedestrian Aberdeen Reservoir Road, which branches off from Mount Cameron Road just behind the garden. Your way lies all downhill from here, along a cool path shaded by trees. Along the way, the track is crossed by Lady Clementi's Ride – a bridle path named after a former governor's wife – which is now part of the Hong Kong Trail. At this juncture bear right by staying on the tarmac road.

Later, at the fork in the road, the quickest way down to Aberdeen is to turn right. But carry on straight ahead to make an interesting

Sampan traffic on Aberdeen Harbour

detour over the stone dam of the Aberdeen Upper Reservoir. Here the way ahead is clearly marked. The dam was built in 1931, and it holds back a lake of placid waters surrounded by lush forest. On the far side, take the first right turn onto the Aberdeen Nature Trail and then keep bearing right by staying on the stone laid path. The trail passes through thickets of scrub trees and bushes before delivering you to the dam of the lower reservoir.

After crossing the dam wall turn left. Back on Aberdeen Reservoir Road, above the dam, there's a Country Parks visitor centre behind the fence on your right which contains displays of local history and wildlife. From here the road leads steeply downhill, passing blocks of public housing, and enters Aberdeen proper beside the town's Tin Hau temple, built in 1851. Follow Aberdeen Main Road bearing slightly left and it will bring you to the bus station, where bus No 70 will whisk you in air-conditioned comfort back to Central. If on the other hand you'd like a little more sightseeing, an underpass to the left of the bus station leads to the busy waterfront.

Commencement of the jogger's trail

Bowen Road to Repulse Bay

4 HOURS

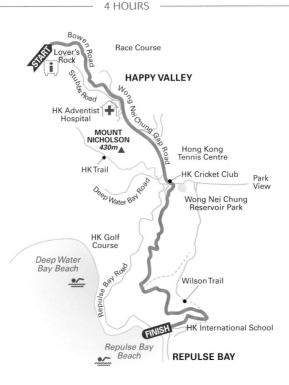

In the same way that Conduit Road began life as an aqueduct, to convey water from Pok Fu Lam Reservoir to the city, so Bowen Road was initially devised to deliver water from Tai Tam. Named after the Governor of the day, it was opened in the 1880s. Its level route, offering city-wide views, can be followed from the Mid-Levels all the way to Wong Nei Chung Gap, and from there across the other side of the island to Repulse Bay or further.

Along the quintessential family hike

Bowen Road starts where Magazine Gap Road is crossed by the Peak Tramway. You can reach this spot by taxi or by taking green minibus 9 from the Star Ferry. The minibus travels down Bowen Road for some way but most of the route is strictly pedestrianised.

A number of attractive old buildings line the initial stretch of the route, and elegant stone retaining walls provide toeholds for impressive banyans. The trail passes beneath the facade of the former Military Hospital, built in 1906 but long superseded by premises in Kowloon. The vacated hospital building is now used as a school.

On the left, a forest of high-rise towers sprout from roots in Central and Wan Chai. Occasional houses still make an appearance on Bowen Road from time

Banyans impart an air of lost Cambodian ruins

to time, even along the sector where vehicle access is prohibited, but as you approach and cross Wan Chai Gap Road, also traffic-free, the surroundings become more untamed.

Be prepared for a pathway on your right. It leads up past a red-hued shrine to Yan Yuen Shek, or Lover's Rock, a place of worship garlanded with seasonal flowers, joss sticks, paper offerings, mirrors and figurines. This phallic monolith, overlooking the harbour, has been popular for many centuries with marriage-minded young women, and as a fertility symbol it still draws devotees.

Bowen Road continues in the direction of Happy Valley, terminating where it meets Stubbs Road. Negotiate the hectic roundabout and follow Wong Nei

Lover's Rock garlanded with ribbon offerings

The city recedes from view as trees take over

Chung Gap Road as it heads gradually uphill. The two tall and impossibly thin towers at the upper end of Happy Valley have already been named "the chopsticks." Walk the pavement on the left, particularly if it's a Sunday, to catch a view of any game in progress at the Hong Kong Cricket Club. Pass the Shell petrol station and take the steps up to Tai Tam Reservoir Road, turning left again to reach the Wong Nei Chung Reservoir.

If in need of refreshment, stop for a drink at the café, and then cross the granite catchment wall of the reservoir. A descent of steps at the other end leads one back into pleasant greenery. Bear right at the fork. This is the Tsz Lo Lan Shan Path, named after the mountain (Violet Hill) it circles. As this is a catchwater trail, it retains a level contour all the way, high above Repulse Bay

Road. Here you are instantly reminded of the tremendous contrast between the heavily urbanised northern flanks of the Hong Kong Island ridgeline and these greener, less intensively developed southern contours. Expansive views open up as one progresses along this walk: Deepwater Bay, Ocean Park, Middle and Lamma islands and beyond. You might almost be in an altogether different geographical setting.

Finally, near the mapboard at Tsin Shui Wan Au, a rough path on the right, which proves a bit of a scramble, leads downhill to the Hong Kong International School at Repulse Bay. Bearing right on South Bay Close takes you towards the beach, restaurants and bus stops.

If your gustatory aspirations are not satisfied at Repulse Bay, you can follow the catchwater for another hour or so as it rounds the southern slopes of Hong Kong Island. The path joins the Wilson Trail as it drops down to Stanley Gap Road, and you can then head into Stanley just in time for a long drink and dinner.

On Sundays – howzat

Through the pass, and the scenery belongs to another world

茶 壺 的 故

Parkland pictures: wedding photos beside the museum

Old Wan Chai and the Flagstaff House Museum of Teaware

1.5 HOURS

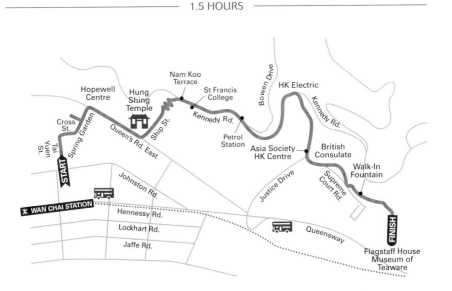

Flagstaff House in Hong Kong Park is our oldest surviving colonial building. On the way there, you can take in some other relics of times gone by.

From Wan Chai MTR station, follow Exit A3 onto Johnston Road. Take the zebra crossing across the tram line, and then make for the side street immediately to the right. This is Tai Yuen Street, entrance to the Wan Chai street market.

Free market: Tai Yuen Street

Signs of a seafaring heritage

Everything is on sale along this pedestrian thoroughfare, from aquarium fish to fresh flowers, children's clothing to jade jewellery. It's usually crowded with shoppers both local and foreign. To the dismay (but not surprise) of many, the government proposes to banish this lively market to a new underground location, and open the street to vehicular traffic, to 'improve the environment'! Most of the buildings behind the market stalls have already been bought up by the Urban Renewal Authority.

Take the first right turn onto Cross Street, and then turn left onto Spring Garden Lane. A 19th-century governor had his mansion here, at a time when this was the waterfront. The area's former close proximity to the sea is recalled in street names like Sampan, Ship and Schooner, and Amoy and Swatow (two Chinese port cities which would have been familiar to coastal sailors).

Soot-blackened altar to Hung Shing

As you reach Queen's Road East, cross over to the other side and turn right, passing the Hopewell Centre. This road is big on furniture shops. Passing the Hung Shing temple (see p.202), take the first left turn. This is Ship Street, and it leads immediately uphill on wide flagstone steps.

The condemned buildings on the left have recently been demolished, revealing the foundations and brick arches of much older structures behind and beneath them. Several foundation stones are inscribed with their original I.L. (inland lot) number. The stone retaining walls high above, capped by balustrades and abundant greenery, are all that remains of the old Tung Chi College. Its name can still be seen painted on one wall. This area of historic ruins, granite steps and well-established wall trees is a reminder of a time when quality materials were used for building – and it's all under threat from Gordon Wu's planned 'Mega Tower' project.

The Hung Shing temple stands on the original shoreline

Splendid survivor: Nam Koo Terrace

High up at the top of Ship Street, one century-old mansion survives.
The red-brick Nam Koo Terrace is built in grand style, with pillars two
storeys high, and must once have had a marvellous sea view. In spite of
its abandoned state, its front courtyard still retains a stone fountain and
pergola. What splendid parties they must have had here in the 1920s!

Where the steps split into three narrower flights, take the middle flight to the right of the red fire hydrant (the other routes up are blocked at the top). You emerge onto Kennedy Road. Carry on in the direction you are facing, passing St. Francis Canossian College and following the paper-bark trees past the turning for Monmouth Path.

Banyan roots find routes to water

There is a small sitting-out area here on Kennedy Road, looking down a steep slope lush with trees. Squirrels can be seen in the branches. Beneath a gnarled banyan, a fallen sign still reads 'Ministry of Defence Property', nearly 30 years after the military handed this area over to the Hong Kong government. As you walk on, you can catch glimpses of a group of former military buildings which were not incorporated into Hong Kong Park: these were explosives magazines which are now being renovated for use by the Asia Society, a cultural organization.

Long-lived granite stairways

A little further on, the perimeter wall of this compound reaches the road. Mind the oncoming traffic here. Take the steps down beside a stream to reach the entrance. Inside, there are tram lines for moving wagons of explosives

Who goes there – friend or foe?

Falling fountain: walk-in cooler

Intelligent design: shuttered verandahs cool the rooms behind

The perfect cup of tea

around. Mounds of earth were placed between the three buildings to temper the effect of any explosions. An anchor sign on the gatepost would seem to mark the site as property of the Admiralty, which gave its name to the district below.

Follow the track downhill, past other long-disused army buildings, and turn left beside the British Consulate. The entrance to Hong Kong Park is a little further on, heralded by a walk-in fountain which provides a great way to cool off. Flagstaff House can be found a little to the right of the main gate. Built in 1846 and used as the residence of the Commander of British Forces, it was handed over to the Hong Kong government in 1978 along with the rest of Victoria Barracks. It now houses a collection of teaware, and holds exhibitions on ceramic art and the culture of tea drinking. Entry is free, and it's open from 10:00am to 5:00pm daily except Tuesdays.

The building is a fine example of tropical colonial architecture: the shuttered verandahs are deep, allowing cool air to circulate. A small arts bazaar is held outside on weekends, and there is a Chinese teahouse in the K. S. Lo Gallery next door.

Finish your walk with alfresco dinner or drinks at L16 Restaurant, beside the park's landscaped lakes, or head for Pacific Place and any of the hotels above it.

Lonely monuments to long-forgotten battles

Happy Valley

2 HOURS

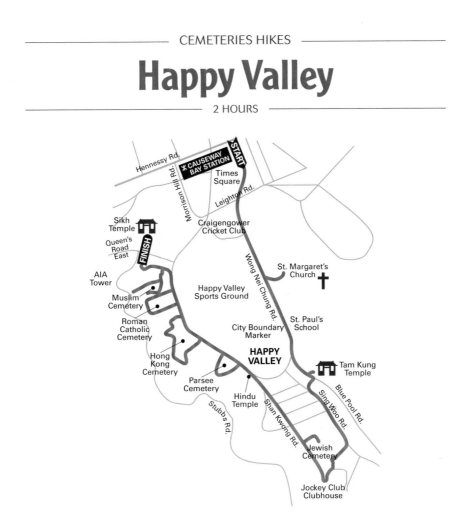

Early colonial town planning called for Happy Valley to be developed into Hong Kong's main business district, but the planners failed to take the deadly malarial conditions of the then swampy marshland into account. Whoever built a house there soon succumbed to fever and perished. The area was thus abandoned for settlement, and cemeteries and a racecourse were laid out instead. These graveyards still remain today, and their inscriptions reveal thought-provoking details about life in Hong Kong from the early 19th century onwards.

Peter and Paul stand sentinel

Travel by MTR to Causeway Bay and leave by Exit A, emerging onto street level amid a crush of direction-challenged shoppers at Times Square. Bear immediately left to walk over to Matheson Street, where you should make a right to reach Leighton Road. Cross over to join Wong Nei Chung Road, keeping the Craigengower Cricket Club on your right, and follow the route of the tram line ahead.

Gothic engraving

Far from the 'yellow muddy stream' which its name describes, Wong Nei Chung Road is lined with bespoke shoe shops, furniture showrooms, delicatessens and ostentatious apartment blocks. It's a prosperous part of town. On your right, two great old banyan trees were moved to their current position in 1995 when the racecourse beyond them was expanded. On the left, St. Margaret's Church overlooks the racecourse from a hill on Broadwood Road. It was built in 1925, and was at that time a very visible local landmark. Its portico features statues of St. Peter and St. Paul.

Nuns and their charges

Further along, a bricked-in archway inscribed 'Le Calvaire' was the entrance to an orphanage opened by French nuns at the turn of the century. The stone frontage is now the foundations of St. Paul's School, still associated with the Order of St. Paul of Chartres. Opposite, a granite boundary stone dated 1903 marks the limits of the city.

Granite marker

Passing the long-established Amigo restaurant, turn left past the bus station onto Blue Pool Road. At the next turning, steps lead up to a Tam Kung temple which is hidden by trees and often overlooked even by local residents. It's built in a partly open-sided style and dates back to 1901, although it was renovated to the tune of HK$2 million in 2006. The busiest time here is during the Tam Kung Festival in the fourth lunar month. Behind it there's a small Tin Hau temple with a very cheerful goddess.

Amply-adorned Tin Hau

Returning to the road, turn left and take Tsoi Tak Street, easily found by the giant Happy Foot sign, and turn left onto Sing Woo Road. This is the heart of Happy Valley and the location of the original Wong Nei Chung village. Happy Valley residents often speak approvingly of their area's 'village atmosphere' – looking around, there are few chain stores but plenty of locally-run wine shops, florists, cheesecake cafés and upscale eateries, so the claim has some truth. The side streets still hide many old-style walk-up buildings.

Elaborate eaves: Chinese roof design

Hebrew inscriptions in the Jewish Cemetery

Turn right after the blue-and-grey police station onto Kwai Fong Street, and enter the small park at the end. Follow the steps up to reach the Hong Kong Jockey Club's plush Happy Valley Clubhouse on Shan Kwong Road. This was originally the location of the club's stables, but the clip-clop of hooves can now be heard only in Sha Tin. On your right as you descend the steep street is the distinctive Tung Lin Kok Yuen, a red-brick Buddhist temple built by Robert Hotung in 1935 and used as a school. Even more ornate buildings next door are used for primary classes.

Between the two sets of buildings, a lane leads into the Jewish Cemetery, laid out in 1855 when its surroundings high up in the valley were entirely rural. It's a quiet spot with few visitors in evidence, although pebbles are left on some of the graves in the Jewish tradition. Familiar Hong Kong names on the headstones include members of the Belilios, Sassoon and Kadoorie families.

Parsee plots are lovingly tended

Follow the road downhill now to its meeting with the tram line, and bear left. There's a Hindu temple just past the Sanatorium, and beside this you'll find the entrance to the Parsee Cemetery. Laid out in 1852, the grounds are well planted. The Parsees were Indian merchants of the Zoroastrian faith who followed the British to Canton. Tombs here include those of such notables as Dorabji Naorojee, founder of the Star Ferry, and Hormusjee Naorojee Mody, who financed the opening of Hong Kong University.

As you leave, you're facing the main entrance to the racecourse. Carry on down the road, passing under a flyover to find the unobtrusive gate to the Hong Kong Cemetery (known before the handover as the Colonial Cemetery). This is a sprawling garden which extends deep into fingers of the valley in all directions, paths partly overgrown and hidden by tall old trees. Little has changed here since 1845 besides the opening of the Aberdeen Tunnel. There are large monuments to army regiments and naval detachments which suffered losses due to military action, pirates or tropical diseases, but some of the more moving headstones are the smaller ones – to Protestant men and women of all nationalities – some of whom died at a very young age and far from home. There are policemen, missionaries, sailors' wives, lords, merchants and teachers, represented by an eclectic range of headstones, with various crosses, urns, pedestals, columns and other decorative details popular at the time. Some tombs give you cause to wonder, such as that of a 22-year-old Japanese officer inscribed in French.

Many of Hong Kong's earliest personalities, such as Catchick Paul Chater, Robert Hotung, Karl Gutzlaff and Granville Sharp are buried here; as you wander the peaceful pathways, you may recognize the origin of several street names on the headstones.

Dorabji Naorojee: ferry founder

Sir Catchick Paul Chater

Next door, St. Michael's Roman Catholic Cemetery is packed into a much tighter space. Names here are predominantly French, Irish, Italian and Portuguese, and many religious orders – the Jesuits, Canossians and so on – have areas to themselves. Perhaps the best-known grave is that of Linda Lin Dai, the most popular film actress of her day, who committed suicide in mysterious circumstances in 1964.

To complete the set of religious denominations, the Muslim Cemetery is found just further on, opposite the Cosmopolitan Hotel. In keeping with Islamic principles it's more austere than the others, with stones inscribed in Chinese, Roman and Arabic scripts but with little adornment.

Terraced tombs: space is tight in the Catholic Cemetery

Islamic idyll: a quiet corner above Wan Chai

The cemeteries are all overlooked by the AIA Tower, which must have the worst feng shui of any office building in Hong Kong; although in true Chinese pragmatic style, the negative forces have been inverted to bring fortune, if the company's apparent success is anything to go by. For a brief detour, Hau Tak Lane leads from the gate of the Muslim Cemetery to the entrance to Hong Kong's Sikh Temple. The rambling building was originally erected in 1901 by Sikh soldiers, but was bombed several times during the Second World War and rebuilt afterwards.

If you're flagging, the Cosmopolitan Hotel has a bar and restaurant. Otherwise, take the underpass across to the other side of Wong Nei Chung Road and follow the signs back to the MTR.

Final tribute from the Police Force

The Inter-Island Ferry

AN ALL-DAY EXCURSION

Ferries are a cheap and enjoyable way to get around Hong Kong, and provide some of the SAR's best views. One vessel has the duty of linking the isles of Peng Chau and Cheung Chau with two locations on Lantau Island, and it travels all day on the same route. Jump on board for a whistle-stop tour of the Western Harbour.

Time out: escape Central for a day amid the islands

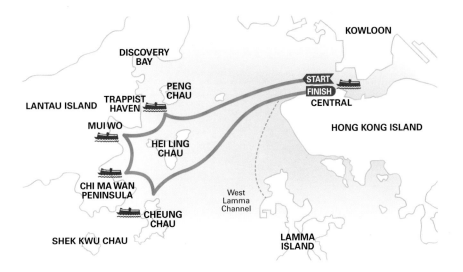

To start, take the Peng Chau-bound ferry from Pier 6 in Central. There are departures roughly every 45 minutes. The 10:00am sailing (or 10:20am on Sundays) will drop you off on Peng Chau for 11:00am. The island is a small commuter settlement with villages, temples and organic farms. You can make an easy circuit to take in its attractions – see p.28 for a suggested route.

Returning to the pier, it's time to catch the Inter-Island Ferry. Other boats do call in at Peng Chau – one for Discovery Bay and the Trappist Monastery, and one for the rehabilitation centre on neighbouring Hei Ling Chau – but the first docks at the nearby public pier, and the other uses an adjacent wharf, so there is little chance of catching the wrong boat. The ferry departs at 1:40pm.

Racing to the ferry

Low-rise Peng Chau, high-rise Discovery Bay

Fisherman zips through Peng Chau waters

Sailing south beside the steep Lantau coast, the ferry rounds the cape at Man Kok Tsui, where large quantities of Bronze Age artefacts have been discovered buried under sand bars. In those times, southern China was inhabited by the Yueh tribes. Silvermine Bay opens up on your right, and the ferry soon docks at the Mui Wo pier. Alight here for a two-hour stopover.

Mui Wo dragonhead

Turning right as you exit the pier, follow the path around to the sandy shore, where the Silvermine Beach Hotel overlooks the water. It's a shallow bay, and villagers collect shellfish at low tide. You can walk all the way to the north end of the beach; some houses and the Mui Wo Inn have lovely views out to sea.

Cascade flows down from the silver mines

Fallow fields of Mui Wo villages

Into the valley, buzzing with cicadas and unseen birds

On your way back, cross the bridge over the creek, and then turn immediately right beside the Silvermine Beach Hotel to move inland. Turn right again as you reach the village houses, following the stream until you reach a fork in the path, where you should turn left. This quiet route leads over a hill and down the other side to reach a bridge over a stream. Cross it and walk upstream a short distance. You'll find a small waterfall and a pavilion beside it. Above this, the hills hide several entrances to the silver mine which once provided employment to the area, but they have been blocked for safety.

Walk back and follow the main path into Pak Ngan Heung ("White Silver Village"). The village is preceded by its Man Mo temple, dedicated to the gods of literature and war. It was likely built in the 17th century, and looks out across a mostly overgrown valley which is flat and fertile, and would once have been intensively farmed.

Searching for silver?

Verdant view from the Man Mo temple

From the far side of the village square, a closed road leads gently downhill to the main town, and then back to the ferry pier. Look out for the Li family boundary stone in a garden between the bus rank and the HSBC – it dates back to Sung dynasty times and was discovered in 1955. Together with another found at Man Kok Tsui, and others lost to history, the stones marked the limits of the large estate granted to Li Mao-ying by the emperor in 1265.

If you have time before your onward sailing, you can grab a bite to eat at any of the cafés nearby. The inter-island ferry leaves at 4:00pm from the right-hand side of the Mui Wo pier.

Twenty minutes at sea brings you to Chi Ma Wan. There is a very small settlement here, and a detention camp which was once used to house Vietnamese boat people. If you decide to alight at this point, you can follow the quiet road over the hill to Pui O, where there is a grand beach and buses to Mui Wo and Tung Chung. Otherwise, stay on board.

Gods of literature and war

Sung-dynasty boundary stone

Crashing ocean waves off Shek Kwu Chau

Island watersports

Boats and banquets

At anchor: Cheung Chau's crowded harbour

The next stop is Cheung Chau, the boat pulling in to the busy harbour just before 5:00pm. There's time for a quick walk around the island (see page 134) before returning to the waterfront for dinner at an open-air restaurant. Ferries run back to Central all evening.

This is a suggested schedule only, and other sailings come and go at different times – pick up a timetable pamphlet at the Central pier. Variations on the route could include walking south along the coast from Silvermine Bay, picking up the ferry again at Chi Ma Wan; or starting from Cheung Chau and taking a sampan or kaido across to Tai Long village or the Sea Ranch resort on Lantau, from where trails lead over the hilly, forested peninsula to the Chi Ma Wan pier.

Yau Ma Tei and its Markets

2 HOURS

Some ancient gems lie hidden in the crowded streets of Kowloon –
and they're not all in the Jade Market. Follow this urban route to discover
temples, teahouses, opera singers and some of Kowloon's oldest
remaining architecture.

Temple Street; jam-packed with shoppers every evening

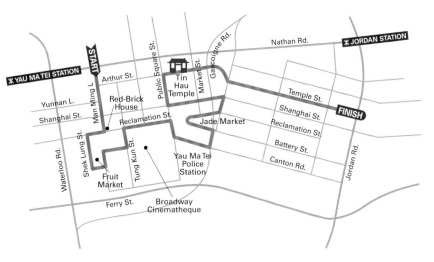

Take the MTR to Yau Ma Tei, leaving the station by Exit C. Crossing Arthur Street puts you on Man Ming Lane. With your back to Nathan Road, walk forwards and make a right turn into the lane directly after the newly-laid garden. These few blocks have recently been demolished and soaring towers have replaced the condemned buildings – the only one to remain is the lone-standing colonial red-brick house on the corner of Shek Lung Street. Built in 1895, it was originally the engineer's office for a pumping station.

Red-brick survivor

Cross Shanghai Street at the corner of Waterloo Road, and then pass through another alley to reach Reclamation Street. The long white building on your right is an abandoned theatre. Over the road lies the old Kowloon fruit market. Step in to have a look around. It's a whirl of activity at five in

The fruit market is sprouting its own blossoms

the morning, when tattooed youths push around wooden trolleys laden with oranges, mangoes and smelly durian, but in the daytime it's left to dozing dogs. Above the shopfronts, stucco Chinese characters proclaim the names of the original fruit laans which traded from these crumbling premises – perhaps the modern occupants are one and the same.

Return to Reclamation Street and turn right, dodging wooden pallets and boxes of fruit. This road and the parallel Shanghai Street were once major commercial thoroughfares of Kowloon, and losing that status to Nathan Road means that many older buildings and shops remain. Take the first right turn into Tung Kun Street. Many roads in the district were named after places in China, but the early Romanizations used render their names meaningless to most Western visitors. This street is named after Dongguan, just over the border.

An open plaza on your left bears the entrance to the Broadway Cinematheque, Hong Kong's biggest arthouse cinema, along with a café and art bookshop. The far end of the plaza opens onto Public Square Street; on the other side of the road, you can see the graceful Yau Ma Tei Police Station, which dates from 1922.

Fruit vendors with seasonal produce

Arthouse cinema

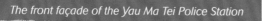

The front façade of the Yau Ma Tei Police Station

Jade, the stone of immortality

Cross the road here and go straight ahead along Canton Road, keeping the colonnaded police station on your right. The Jade Market appears a few minutes later, hidden under a flyover on Battery Street. All shades and qualities of jade and jadeite are on sale here. The bangles and trinkets make great gifts, and bargaining is the time-honoured way to buy. The market is divided into two sections and is open until 6:00pm.

Exiting the second half of the market, turn left. This returns you to Public Square Street, where you should turn right, crossing Shanghai Street once again to meet the curios stalls of the Temple Street night market. Business starts up in the late afternoon. The Mido Café, a teahouse which retains the atmosphere of 1960s Hong Kong, occupies the corner on the far left. Why not stop for a cup of lai cha? Enjoying the evening sun through its first-floor windows is a great way to prepare for a film at the nearby cinema or a night of shopping.

Bangles, beads and bargains

The illuminated night market

The ancient Tin Hau Temple at the back of the square, partly veiled by trees, once stood on the seashore – all this land is reclaimed. Its goddess looks after seafarers but it is many years since the temple had a view of the sea. Today, the banyan-shaded square is occupied by old men playing cards and Chinese checkers, and other characters engaged in less innocent activities; the various vice trades are as active in Yau Ma Tei today as they ever have been.

Walk across to the square's southern side: here you will find fortune tellers operating from tables on the pavement. Each has a different method of divining destiny. One reads hands or faces; another relies on a small finch to pick the correct sticks from a selection laid before it. Some of these soothsayers speak English and you can negotiate a price for looking into your future.

Tin Hau lintel and welcoming entrance

Divining the future

Brush and ink with geomancer's theories

If you are in luck, a Cantonese opera troupe may be practising their notes on the pedestrianized section of Market Street to your left. The singing sounds odd to Western ears but follows an ancient tradition. If you listen for a while, you're expected to throw a few coins in the collection plate to support the troupe's work.

Pass under the flyover which emerges bizarrely from the side of a building. From here, the night market carries on down the length of Temple Street. As well as shopping for clothes and gifts, you can stop for dinner or drinks at a number of local restaurants and food stalls along the way. Signs will point you back to the MTR at Jordan; or, if you prefer, you can follow Temple Street all the way to Kowloon Park, and make your way through its grounds to reach Tsim Sha Tsui.

Stage make-up prior to the performance

Well-tended gardens honour those who fell long ago in the defence of Hong Kong

Stanley

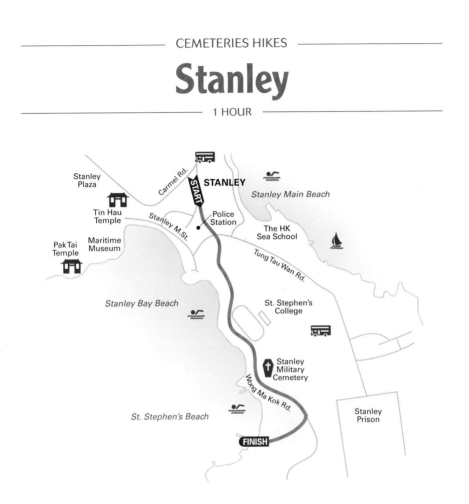

Perhaps due to its large army base, or air defences – or maybe due to a simple accident of geography – Stanley was a major battlefield in the Second World War. In fact, the British forces made their last stand here in December 1941. Stanley Fort still occupies the southern portion of the peninsula, and many of Hong Kong's fallen soldiers are laid to rest in the Military Cemetery.

Take bus 6, 6X or 260 from Exchange Square in Central, alighting at the bus station. Walk ahead, in the direction of the old police station. For many years used as an upscale restaurant, and now a supermarket, it was built in 1859 and is the oldest remaining police station in Hong Kong.

Rough-hewn markers rest under the trees

Heritage tour pauses among the headstones

Continue south along Wong Ma Kok Road, passing the playing fields of St. Stephen's College, used as a civilian internment camp during the war. The cemetery appears shortly thereafter on your left. It's a nicely shaded spot sometimes used for picnics. Many of the graves date from the earliest days of colonial Hong Kong, and although some of the inscriptions record those who fell victim to skirmishes with pirates, others mark those who died from malaria. In those days, Hong Kong had a reputation as a noxious place where life was short, and more soldiers were lost to mosquitoes than to enemy action.

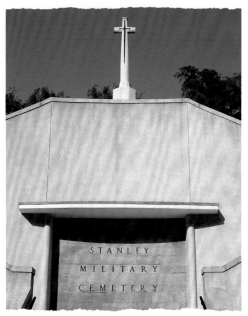

Honourable resting place for Hong Kong's defenders

Skipping between the beaches at St. Stephen's

Candy-coloured sails unfurl at St Stephen's

Deserted beaches offer time for rest and reflection

Leaving the cemetery, take the lane which leads down to the pleasantly uncrowded St. Stephen's Beach – a good weekend alternative to Stanley Main Beach for those reluctant to share the sands with the entire population of Causeway Bay. It's home to a watersports centre, and windsurfers can usually be watched learning the ropes. If the time is right, you may also see the old Po Toi ferry creaking beside the pier. The wooden vessel makes the journey to the sparsely-populated island just three times a week.

Looking out to sea, try to imagine the heavy drumbeats which would have resounded across the water, calling Cheung Po-tsai's pirate ships to action. The notorious nineteenth-century bandit used Stanley's Tin Hau temple as a signalling station. Today, the residents of Stanley still beat drums, but nowadays they mark time for dragonboat races.

If you walk to the north end of the beach, over the rocks, you can take a narrow stairway back up to Wong Ma Kok Road. Turn left to return to Stanley Market and a diversity of dinner options.

Stanley: liquid luncheon locale

Souvenir market

Waterfront strip is Stanley's dining destination

Octagonal design for a city temple

Lin Fa Kung and Tin Hau

1 HOUR

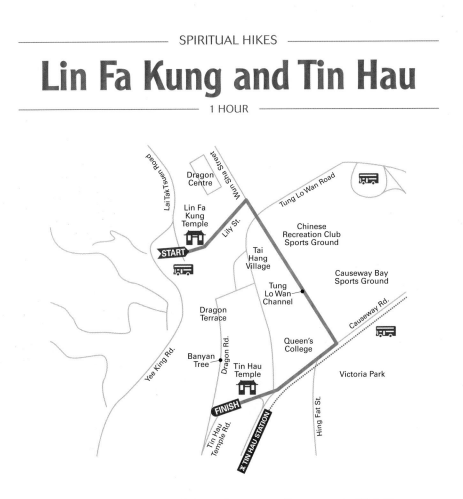

Take bus 23A or 26, or a taxi, from Causeway Bay up to Lai Tak Tsuen. Disembark at the terminus. It's a typical public housing estate which shares harbour views with the posh residences of Jardine's Lookout.

From the sleepy bus station, steps lead down to a garden in which stands the Lin Fa Kung. Unlike other Chinese temples, which generally keep to a set design, this one is architecturally unique, being octagonal in shape. It is dedicated to Kwun Yam. The main altar is beautifully detailed, overseen by a friendly, English-speaking guardian of the temple.

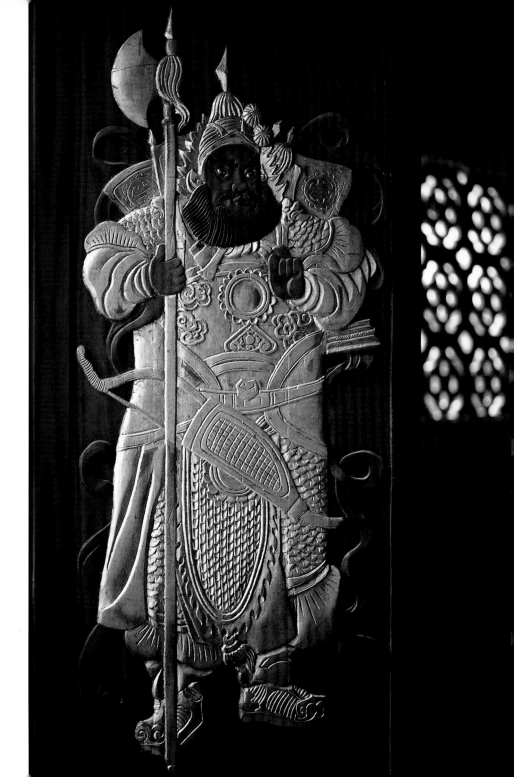

Gilded Guardians

Giant incense coils suspended above the altar at Lin Fa Kung

The gully and path beside the playing fields

Following Lily Street brings you into the old neighbourhood known as Tai Hang Village. These streets play host to the annual Fire Dragon Dance, a well-attended event which is held around the time of the Mid-Autumn Festival. The ceremony commemorates a nineteenth-century outbreak of plague which was eradicated after a goddess appeared to the villagers and instructed them to perform the dance. In thanks, or perhaps in acknowledgement of the truth that prevention is better than cure, it has been performed annually ever since. Walk further along Lily Street and turn right.

Lacquered lanterns cast a welcoming glow

The name Tai Hang refers to a large watercourse which used to empty into the sea near here; Wun Sha Street recalls the washing of clothes on the banks of the stream. Follow this street to where it meets Tung Lo Wan Road ("Tung Lo Wan" is the Chinese name for Causeway Bay). Here, a channelled remnant of the stream still passes through the grounds of Queen's College. Follow this northwards, away from the road.

The old boys of Queen's College

Queen's College dates from the earliest days of colonial Hong Kong, and has stood on this site since 1950. Its open playing fields – which have been used for much longer, since 1897 – provide a welcome contrast to the nearby crush of Yee Wo Street.

A pantheon of spiritual characters occupies the roof ridge

Red lantern for joy

Stone lion guards the temple's precincts

Emerging onto Causeway Road opposite Victoria Park, you should turn right. Note the nineteenth-century cannons outside the entrance to the college. Cross Tung Lo Wan Road and walk uphill on Tin Hau Temple Road. A short rise brings you to an old but well-kept Tin Hau temple, built on a stone platform. Like all shrines to the goddess of seafarers, this one used to be on the coast, but reclamation has pushed it far inland. It's a busy location; in fact its popularity is such that it has given its name to the whole district.

Here too is a conveniently located public toilet. Step onto Dragon Terrace, on the slope above, to see one of Hong Kong's champion banyan trees, on its own island directly in the middle of the road. Finish off by retracing your steps downhill to reach buses, trams or the MTR.

MISCELLANEOUS

Tsing Yi and the Tsing Ma Bridge

2 HOURS

When Hong Kong's islands got together to draw lots for their fortunes, Tsing Yi picked the short straw. Located opposite the industrial suburb of Tsuen Wan, the island's shores were reclaimed from the 1950s onwards and developed into shipyards, power stations and oil depots. In more recent times, it has been colonized by housing estates and container terminals, and used as a transit point by the airport railway and its associated bridges and tunnels. But despite all this development, the highland areas of the island remain untouched, and a nature trail can be followed which gives spectacular close-up views of the Tsing Ma bridge.

Glittering panorama: a jewelled ribbon of moving lights links Kowloon to Lantau

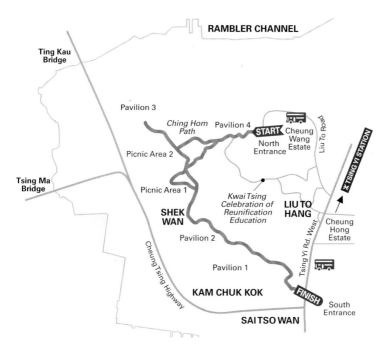

Shipyards and housing line the Rambler Channel

Three islands joined by two bridges

Take the Tung Chung MTR line to Tsing Yi station. The ticket barriers lead out into the Maritime Square shopping mall. Follow the bus/taxi signs down to level One, and leave by Exit A1 for the bus terminus, which is reached by footbridge. This is a part of Tsing Yi densely packed with residential towers. This area was in fact originally Nga Ying Chau – an offshore islet once Hong Kong's smallest inhabited island. Before reclamation, the channel between Nga Ying Chau and Tsing Yi was crammed with sampans and stilt houses.

Bear left to reach the stop for bus 248M, or descend by stairs to the taxi rank. Either way, your destination is Cheung Wang Chuen, a 15-minute ride away. If you arrive by taxi, you can be dropped off directly at the north entrance to the nature trail – otherwise it's a brief walk up Liu To Road from the bus station.

The trail was laid out in 1998, just after the opening of the airport connection, and is easy to follow. Take the steps uphill. You're immediately enveloped by greenery. Go straight ahead at the first pavilion, and then turn right at the fork onto Ching Hom Path. You arrive at a picnic area at a T-junction, where an opening straight ahead through the bush provides the first views of the Tsing Ma bridge. Here, you're lined up with both towers, and looking straight down the span of the giant bridge to Ma Wan and Lantau on the other side.

It's the world's longest double-decker suspension bridge, vaulting a 2.2-kilometre gap between islands, and carrying road and rail traffic on separate levels. With a price tag of HK$7 billion, it was among the costliest components of the infrastructure needed to replace the former airport at Kai Tak with a larger twin-runway airport at Chek Lap Kok. Together with the connecting Ting Kau and Kap Shui Mun bridges, it links Hong Kong and the New Territories to the new airport.

The bridge was inaugurated by Margaret Thatcher in April 1997 to the accompaniment of fireworks and a laser show, and it is illuminated nightly to striking effect. The lights are turned on at 6:00pm from October to February and at 7:30pm from March to September. If you come to see this, remember to bring a torch, as you'll be returning downhill in the dark.

Moving on, take the right-hand turn at this T-junction to reach another pavilion on a spur. This one overlooks the neighbouring Ting Kau bridge. Tree cover has increased since the trail was laid out, and you can now catch only a glimpse through the branches. There is however a clear view of the Rambler Channel, and Tsuen Wan beyond it.

The mighty span bridges a 2.2km gap between islands

The Ting Kau bridge was built to an untested design, and the question was whether its central tower would prove strong enough to sustain the tremendous loads placed on it. The cable-stayed system resembles a sailboat rig: cables running from the central tower mast to the outer ends of a cross strut under the road decks, and then in again to grip the tower footings. The longitudinal stay cables are the longest ever installed on a bridge. Scepticism was voiced as to the outcome, but when the bridge was opened in 1998 it elicited nothing but praise, its grace and symmetry far exceeding the more conventional designs of the two neighbouring bridges.

Return to the T-junction and go straight ahead, bearing right at the first fork to reach another picnic area with a different perspective on the Tsing Ma bridge. Even before illumination, this point provides a dramatic view, as swooping suspension cables are silhouetted against water turned gold by the setting sun. It's well recommended to time this hike for sunset, and to give yourself enough time to find the best vantage point. The nearest tower of the bridge stands on the site of Wok Tai Wan, a once-secluded bay which was used as a nudist colony in the 1950s.

The trail continues southwards over the ridge of the hills, providing changing views of the bridges and surrounding coastlines until it drops into a wooded valley to meet Tsing Yi Road West. Turn left to walk along to the bus stop near Cheung Hong Estate; buses run from here back to Tsing Yi MTR station.

Sailboat rig design of the Ting Kau bridge

The iridescent Ting Kau bridge is the connection between the New Territories and the airport

Sheung Yiu Folk Museum

1.5 HOURS

Deep in the woods of Sai Kung country park, by the shore of the
Pak Tam Chung estuary, lies a tiny walled village. In days gone by,
Hakka villagers used kilns to manufacture bricks, tiles and lime.
This ancient cottage industry died out long ago, and today Sheung Yiu
is a folk museum holding an exhibition of rural life.

Get to Pak Tam Chung by bus 94 from Sai Kung town, or all the way from
Diamond Hill MTR on weekends by bus 96R. Sai Kung town can be reached
by bus 92 from Diamond Hill or minibus 1A from Choi Hung MTR.

The winnowing machine sifted impurities from grain

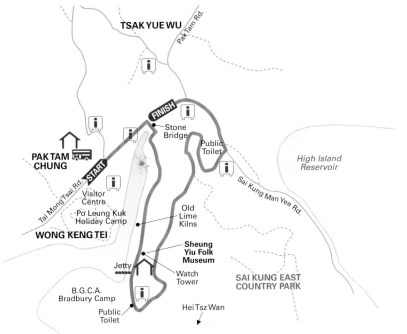

On your marks: Trailwalker teams get going

The bus stops by the country parks visitor centre. The road from here on is barred to general traffic, and only public buses and residents' vehicles may enter the country park. Get off here and have a look at the displays inside the visitor centre – they will give you a broad overview of the culture and geography of Sai Kung.

To start your hike, walk past the country parks road barrier, keeping to the right-hand side of the road. This is in fact the beginning of the 100km MacLehose Trail, and once a year, thousands of people gather at this point to await starter's orders for the Trailwalker hiking event.

In a few minutes, you'll come to an old stone bridge crossing the stream. Note the inscribed plaque recording the names of those who contributed funds towards its construction. Cross over to the other bank and follow the coastal path along to the right.

The Pak Tam Chung stream is wide and shallow here as it approaches the sea. Mangroves thrive in this salty environment. You can also see the pineapple-like fruits of the pandanus plant, which often makes its home by the shore. The fruits stay afloat in water and can drift to new places to take root.

Family walk: on the riverbank

An altar appears by the path, preceded by a stone tablet. This was placed here in 1909 to hold flags and banners. The altar is dedicated to the mountain god Tai Wong Yeh, Sheung Yiu's guardian spirit.

Old bridge funded by villagers' contributions

Lime kiln close to the shore

Entry to the coral-fuelled furnace

Further along, a stone mound protrudes out towards the water. This is one of Sheung Yiu's old lime kilns, built around 1830. Coral and shells were gathered from the sea and burnt inside the chamber. It took several days of wood-fired burning to produce lime, which was then used to make fertilizer and cement. This was an important source of income for coastal communities.

The village itself occupies a raised platform which is a natural defensive position. Abandoned in the 1960s, it has been fully restored and now houses traditional Hakka furniture and farming implements. One such tool is a winnowing machine which generates blasts of air to blow impurities out of falling grain. The watch tower is the only entrance to the village, providing security against bandits and pirates. Inside, eight individual houses open onto a communal courtyard which overlooks the approach path. Indeed, 'Sheung Yiu' means 'above the kiln'. The museum is open until 4:00pm every day except Tuesdays.

Rustic chair fashioned from bamboo

The village jetty still pokes out into the estuary. Once, boats would have called here to load up with lime for export. Now the colourful Po Leung Kuk children's holiday camp is reflected in the still waters.

Walk on until you reach another terrace of old houses still coloured 1960s blue, and swing left at the 'Y' junction to cross a coastal valley. Watch out for concealed field wells beside the meandering path. After crossing a stream, the path climbs quickly up

Side stool in pre-restoration condition

Woodland streams trickle down every rockface

to the beautifully sited village of Hei Tsz Wan. Unlike Sheung Yiu, this settlement has not been restored, and its brightly painted houses are open to the elements. The village is set high above a secluded bay.

Returning to the terrace of houses and turning right, you can make a brief detour to the left to end at a quiet pier with a view of the bay's islands.

Sheung Yiu's jetty for exporting lime

On your way back to Sheung Yiu, and just before you reach it, take the 'family walk' trail which branches off to your right and leads uphill. There's a public toilet here. Go straight ahead at the 'You are here' signboard. Turning left again puts you on a pleasantly natural contour path which has so far escaped the concrete brigade. It ends at the reservoir road. Uphill lies one end of the great High Island Reservoir; but you should coast downhill, arriving very quickly at a road junction. Here you can either turn left to return immediately to the bus station, or turn right and then join the Pak Tam Chung Family Walk on the left, which takes you on a slightly more circuitous route to the same finishing point.

Winding detour to Hei Tsz Wan

Serene surface: High Island Reservoir

Tributary statuary at Che Kung Temple

Che Kung Temple, Tsang Tai Uk and the Hong Kong Heritage Museum

1.5 HOURS

As your border-bound train exits the Lion Rock Tunnel to enter the New Territories, the first part of Sha Tin you see is Tai Wai. Three cultural attractions are found within easy walking distance of this railway station.

Take the KCR to Tai Wai. Leaving by Exit A, turn right and follow the cycle path to reach the Shing Mun River Channel. Turn right again and then aim straight ahead, joining a spur road which leads directly to a pedestrian underpass. The Che Kung Temple is on the other side.

The ubiquitous pink signs clearly mark the way left as you exit the underpass.

Enter the compound through the gateway facing the road. Red-cloaked soothsayers line the wall to your left, while stone guardians occupy the middle ground. It's immediately apparent that this temple is built on a grander scale than usual. Che Kung was a general in the Sung dynasty. According to local legend, he delivered the villagers of Sha Tin from a plague, and since then his temple has been besieged by those seeking similar good fortune. It is particularly busy at Chinese New Year, when thousands of worshippers crowd the temple to wish Che Kung a happy birthday. The Secretary for Home Affairs is the most high-profile visitor at this time; he customarily draws lots to win good luck for the whole of Hong Kong.

Che Kung himself is represented by an enormous and rather angry-looking statue in the main hall. Devotees making offerings at his feet are entitled to turn a wheel and strike a drum for good fortune. On this writer's weekday visit, worshippers ranged from a Canto-pop star to a bus driver.

Granite warrior standing guard

Worshippers ask for Che Kung's guidance

Outside, women sell all types of religious supplies. The complex was greatly expanded in the early 1990s; the original temple is in fact much smaller and hidden behind the main hall.

Facing the altar in the main building, return to the road by the exit on your left and turn right. By the bus stop, take the steps down through an archway marked with the Buddhist swastika. This colourful place has more of a Thai aspect. On a raised platform at the back of the compound, a four-faced Buddha under a jewelled canopy is garlanded with flowers. Take a look inside the hall beside it. Dozens of golden figures line the eaves, as if floating on clouds. The steps behind the hall will lead you back down to the entrance.

Jewelled pavilion for a many-faced Buddha

Hall of golden figures

Hakka architecture: unique corner towers

Turning right again, enter another subway and follow the pink signs for Tsang Tai Uk. Don't take the first turning to the left – proceed straight ahead, then turn right. Carry straight on along the pavement. A little further on, you must descend into yet another convoluted underpass, again clearly signposted in pink for Tsang Tai Uk, and emerge beside the tennis courts. It is a shame that pedestrians are so often forced underground in Hong Kong; perhaps one day they will rise up from their subterranean confines and reclaim the streets from motor traffic.

Tsang Tai Uk lies straight ahead, here signposted by its official name, Shan Ha Wai ("walled village below the mountain"). Apart from the modern windows, it is an incredibly well-preserved fortified village; all the more surprising since it is very much still in use. Three gateways lead into a set of interior courtyards, and an ancestral hall marks the centre of the village. A pair of wells are still used to draw water.

The unusual architectural style of the village is due to the fact that Tsang Koon-man, its Hakka founder, came from an eastern part of Guangdong. He built the village in the mid-19th century to house his clan, but it started to fill up with refugees from China in the late 1940s, and it was they who gave it its current name – Tsang's Great House. Note the tridents atop each corner tower, placed there for feng shui purposes.

At the far end of the village's front yard, turn left at the cow-horned Pak Kung shrine to make a circuit of the green fallow area. From this perspective you can visualize the village in its original setting, surrounded by fields instead of housing estates.

Tsang's Great House

Hand-made costumed puppetry

The Heritage Museum: a huge repository of Hong Kong culture

Returning to the underpass, follow the pink signs now for the Hong Kong Heritage Museum. It's a short walk across the Lion Rock Bridge. The museum is open every day except Tuesdays, and admission is $10. It's a very large building – in fact it is Hong Kong's biggest museum – and is built in traditional style around a central courtyard. Amongst the many exhibition halls you'll find permanent displays on New Territories heritage and the history of Cantonese opera. Try the interactive stage makeup booths to find out what you would look like as an operatic performer.

Cherry-lipped charmer promotes a brand of herbal ointment

Leaving the museum, head for the riverside path and turn right, dodging joggers and cyclists. The tree-shaded path leads past schools and across the river back to Tai Wai Station.

Ancestral altar: family fealty

Lung Yeuk Tau

2 HOURS

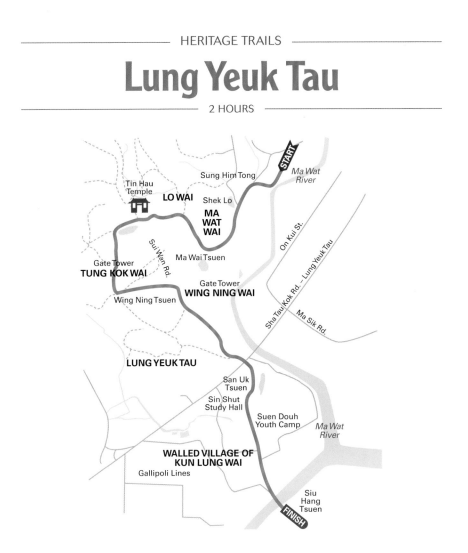

Like the Ping Shan trail, the other officially-sanctioned heritage trail in the New Territories is also based around villages and halls built by a branch of the Tang clan. The Tangs of Lung Yeuk Tau are descended from a princess of the Southern Song dynasty who came to Hong Kong in the 13th century. They established 11 villages, five of them walled, east of current-day Fanling. Though now surrounded by modern three-storey houses, many old structures have survived.

Travel by KCR to Fanling and take the exit for the green minibus station. Here you need to board minibus 54K, which passes by Luen Wo Hui, the traditional marketplace for the area. Alight just after the industrial estate, as the bus crosses a narrow bridge over the Ma Wat river. Ask the driver to drop you off at Sung Him Tong or Lok Tung Gai. Alternatively you can take a green taxi for the brief hop, asking for the same destination.

Over the bridge, the road becomes a single track, and it's here that the heritage trail starts. Don't rely on finding much signage, as there is shockingly little; but the attractions are generally close together and you will soon realise if you have taken a wrong turning.

Glazed ceramics

Private compound: behind the red gate

Passing a toilet block and a kindergarten, you reach the first item on the trail: the cream-coloured church of Shung Him Tong. Built in 1926, it was extended in 1951, at which point the communist stars were presumably added to the edifice; they are a common feature on village houses built in the post-war period, but seem a little odd on a church. Down the alley to the right of the church, a handsome house dating from 1910 is hidden in a compound protected by a red stone gateway.

Further along the road, you should be able to see a fine old mansion hidden in long grass on your right. Built in 1925 by the founder of Wah Yan College, Shek Lo is an elegant combination of Chinese and colonial architecture, but it is currently in an abandoned state.

石廬

Out to pasture: Shek Lo

Safe as houses

Follow the road northwards. A giant banyan with trailing aerial roots welcomes you to Ma Wat Wai. Here you'll find the first walled village on the trail. Built in the 18th century, it has a solid stone gatetower with iron-ring gates. The internal layout of the village is symmetrical; at the back, the village shrine has fallen into disrepair, and now consists of an open-air altar below ivy-covered walls which look as if they could topple over at any moment.

At the crossroads, turn right to reach Lo Wai, another walled village which sits on a raised platform. You need to walk around it to find the entrance. Lo Wai was the first walled structure built by the Tang clan, and its narrow doorway was designed to protect villagers from bandits. There are several old houses inside the walls, plus an old well.

Very close by, the Tang Chung Ling Ancestral Hall sits behind an open plaza. It's one of the largest such halls in the New Territories, with fine wood carvings and murals, and was built in the early 16th century. At the back of the courtyard, a central chamber houses the soul tablets of the Tang ancestors, including that of the Song princess. It's open from 9:00am-1:00pm and 2:00pm-5:00pm, except on Tuesdays. Behind the hall, a small Tin Hau temple has been restored in the same colourful style. Its age is not known, although one of the bronze bells inside is dated 1695.

A mantle of ivy

Breeze can enter, bandits cannot

Weather-worn calligraphy

Hefty walls protect the village from attack

Tang Chung Ling Ancestral Hall

Brackets and rafters in feng shui colours

Rich decorative details

Each village has only one entrance

Family tree: reading the soul tablets

Go straight ahead from the plaza, passing the houses of Tsz Tong Tsuen on your right, until the road curves left to pass a pair of earth god shrines. Bear left at each fork until you reach a playground with banyan trees. Behind this you'll find the gatetower to Tung Kok Wai, another walled village. Its slightly raised position protects the houses inside from seasonal flooding. The tower still has the wooden bars used to close the village after sunset.

Leaving the tower, turn left to follow a winding path between smallholdings. This brings you back to the single-track road, upon which you should turn right. In a few minutes you'll arrive at a basketball court opposite Wing Ning Tsuen. A blue gate allows access into the tree-shaded village courtyard, a good place to stop and eat a packed lunch.

You can turn right to exit the village by its north gate; a little further along the road, you should see the

Antique fresco, awaiting restoration

gatetower to Wing Ning Wai. This is built from unusual red sandstone, and dates from 1744.

A green-tiled pavilion heralds the trail's junction with Sha Tau Kok Road. Cross over and continue on the other side, bearing right into San Uk Tsuen, a confusing muddle of village houses. Here you'll find the grey-brick Sin Shut Study Hall, built in 1840 as a place of learning for clan children. Officially it's not open to the public, but you can step into the courtyard and have a look around.

From here, a path leads in between houses to run beside playing fields – if you can see the blue dorms of the Christian-run Suen Douh youth camp on your left, you're on the right track. On the other side is a children's home run by the Sisters of the Precious Blood, and beyond that, the barracks of Gallipoli Lines – now renamed and occupied by the PLA.

Final fortress: Kun Lung Wai

Entry to the altar

The path leads onto an open area which was originally the moat for the settlement now facing you. This is Kun Lung Wai, the largest walled village on the trail. It has four impressive corner watchtowers, and its entrance is unique in that it is made up of two gatetowers, one behind the other. At the far end of the central alley, preceded by flowers, you'll find the village altar.

The road angles right around Kun Lung Wai and then makes a left turn to cross a bridge. This brings you to Siu Hang Tsuen, which marks the end of the heritage trail. The small village has an archway and low wall built for feng shui purposes. Here you can wait for the green minibus 54C, which will carry you back to Fanling KCR station.

If you have time left over at Fanling, you may like to visit Fung Ying Sin Koon, a popular Taoist temple reached by bridge from the station. Established in 1929, it's a place of traditional eaved halls, glazed murals, ornate decoration and garden pavilions. It also has a vegetarian restaurant – last meals served at 5:00pm.

Arrivals at Lamma's capital city of Yung Shue Wan

Lamma Island

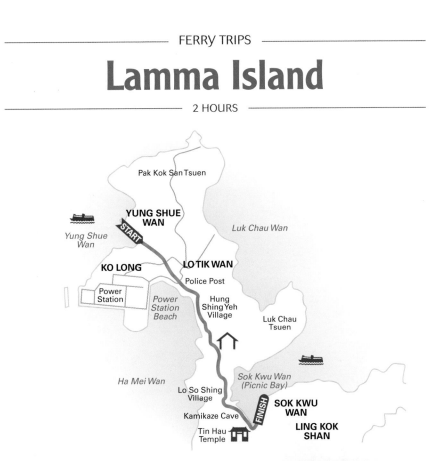

A well-trodden weekend excursion is the walk from one coast of Lamma Island to the other. Both are served by ferries and possess a wealth of restaurants for a post-hike feed. There is no traffic, and a stroll along the spine of the island provides a delightful day out for the social group, the family or the individual.

Board the ferry at Central Pier 4 to Yung Shue Wan (Banyan Tree Bay). It runs frequently and the journey is accomplished in around 25 minutes.

Alfresco restaurants and cafés, Lamma's 'other worldly' qualities

Deeply indented bays, pleasure craft and ideal hiking

Upon arrival, follow the hordes of day-trippers and residents down the pier to Yung Shue Wan Main Street. The once-sleepy village is possibly the most cosmopolitan dormitory suburb in Hong Kong, home to a wide variety of nationalities who prefer the rural environment and cleaner air.

Signs along the street – Deli Lamma, Pizza Milano, Spicy Island, Bali Holiday Resort, Aroy Thai, Bookworm Café, Forget-Me-Not Video, Green Cottage – advertise services suited to its diverse character.

Turn left at the Shell gas shop to join Yung Shue Wan Back Street. The path is lined with makeshift stalls selling handicrafts to weekend visitors. The crowds thin out as fallow fields begin to replace the three-storey villas.

Turn right at a "dau fu fa" (sweet beancurd) café to join a path set above fields on both sides. This leads, finally, through a line of trees, to what is known locally as Power Station Beach. The eponymous power plant aside, the beach enjoys a clear view of the wilder west coast of Lamma Island.

Turning left here, the cement road winds upwards inland. Take the first right past the police post, where bicycles are parked outside. The path opens out onto Hung Shing Yeh beach, manned by lifeguards and hectic at weekends.

The tide rushes in at Hung Shing Yeh beach

Cavia Café and the Concerto Inn serve cold drinks. Carry on past the barbecue pits at its far end. Suddenly the trail shoots uphill, and within a few short minutes, you're high above the western coast. Pleasure boats dot the bay below, and Wailingding, a Chinese island, sits on the horizon. Mount Stenhouse, Lamma's highest peak, looms heavily to the south.

The path dips through a couple of valleys before reaching a well-used lookout pavilion. From this midpoint of the hike you're able to look back at the outskirts of Yung Shue Wan.

Shortly the central ridge of the island is crossed and Sok Kwu Wan (or Picnic Bay) appears below, busy with fish culture rafts. Seafood restaurants line the far shore. The next stop is Lo So Shing Village, a quiet settlement of traditional houses with firewood stacked for fuel. The path swings right, then left, and then left again at a fork which otherwise leads downhill to the pleasant but less visited Lo So Shing beach. Our path leads on past the village school and the "kamikaze caves", which provided hiding places for Japanese patrol boats awaiting an invasion at the end of the Second World War.

It's easy going now around the shallow estuary. At low tide, you can take a direct route across the mudflats to the open ground in front of the Tin Hau temple. The temple is well-kept and worth a look. Walking through Sok Kwu Wan means running a gauntlet of over-eager restaurant staff, all intent on diverting you to one of their outdoor tables. Mind you don't stumble into a bubbling tank of seafood as you pick your way through the crowds.

Ferries for Central and Aberdeen leave from two separate ferry piers. The journey to Aberdeen is more of an adventure, since you can sit on the prow of the wooden vessel as it crosses the East Lamma Channel.

This hike can be extended by either continuing along the coastal path to Mo Tat Wan, a quiet seaside settlement, and picking up the Aberdeen ferry from there; or by taking the stairs uphill from the Tin Hau temple, a longer detour which passes the sheltered Tung O ("Eastern Cove") before approaching Mo Tat Wan from the south.

The colourful temple of Sok Kwu Wan

Always room for one more – the Aberdeen ferry

Shek O

Hong Kong's biggest rollers crash onto the sands of Shek O and Big Wave Bay, at the far eastern limits of the island. The coast is rocky and untamed, and not until 1923 did this peninsula become accessible by road. No longer do ancient China Motor Bus "boneshakers" make the hairpin-edged journey; these days six-wheeled leviathans speed hordes of bathers to the beach, and the margin of error for spectacular accidents must have narrowed – but only slightly.

Shek O, the island's most remote extremity

Tidal waters and rustic coast of the headland

Take the MTR to Shau Kei Wan and leave the station by Exit A3, boarding the no. 9 bus at the far end of the bus rank. Or, if it's Sunday, catch the 309 from Exchange Square. Take a top-deck seat if possible to enjoy the white-knuckle ride. Once the bus reaches Shek O Road, views of Tai Tam Harbour open up far below. There is a stop at the quarry on Windy Gap. Then it's all downhill to the coast, passing villas and fairways as you go.

The bus sometimes stops at the art deco-style bus terminus and sometimes directly in front of the beach itself. Policemen wave away private cars; there's no more room, the beach is full. Enter the ramshackle village by way of the traffic roundabout. Shek O seems to have grown without any regard to town planning, and as a result has an accidental charm not unlike the fishing villages of the outlying islands. There is a Tin Hau temple hidden amongst

The village's own Tin Hau temple

the alleys, nestled beside bohemian restaurants and houses groaning under the weight of flowerpots. Follow the road as it winds its way slowly uphill. More substantial houses exist here on the headland, hidden behind high walls and highly sought after.

The road comes to an end facing the offshore islet of Tai Tau Chau, to which a blue-grey bridge provides access over low-tide rocks. Take any path; they diverge but all meet again at the green pagoda at the top. You're given a good view back at Shek O, the beach jam-packed with sun-worshippers. It's all open sea to the east. The white-painted headland on your left belongs to Tung Lung Chau, popular with rock climbers. Far to the south, the lighthouse on Waglan Island can be seen guarding the furthest extremity of Hong Kong waters.

The tide observed from a safe distance

The little community of Shek O is largely Arcadian

Return to the village the way you came, but bear right through the maze of passageways to Rocky Bay. An open-air beach bar is a favourite sundowner spot for expat residents. The pastel-pink gateway to the village clinic provides a short cut back to the main road.

After a swim at the main beach, treat yourself to a meal and a thirst-quencher at one of the many Thai or Chinese restaurants lining the street. Buses 9, 309 or itinerant red minibuses afford varying degrees of peril on the run back to town.

On weekends Shek O is inundated by incursions of city folk

Harbour gap: the narrowest point between Hong Kong and Kowloon

-- KOWLOON --

Lei Yue Mun

-- 2.5 HOURS --

Lei Yue Mun is the narrowest stretch of Victoria Harbour. Sandwiched by high peaks, it's a natural defensive position, and colonial forts and batteries were built on both sides. This hike barely leaves Kowloon but benefits from great sea views and finishes amongst village seafood restaurants. A note of caution; avoid the Ching Ming and Chung Yeung Festivals when untold numbers of visitors honour ancestral graves.

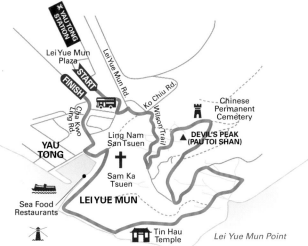

Take the MTR to the spacious, canary-yellow Yau Tong Station. It overlooks old sawmills on the waterfront and is the nearest point to the start of Section 3 of the Wilson Trail, which can be tricky to find. The most straightforward way is to leave by Exit A2; descend the stairs, go straight ahead and turn left onto Ko Chiu Road; pass the roundabout; and then take the second turning on the right. It's signposted only for the Chinese Permanent Cemetery.

Alternatively leave by Exit A2; turn left and pass the satirical *'Ladies Lazing'* sculpture by Li Wei-han, winner of *'Artist of the Year Award 1999'*, and take the escalator up to Lei Yue Mun Plaza, clearly signposted. Then turn right and first left, to the busy Lei Yue Mun Road. Cross over at the traffic signal; turn right to the roundabout where directions to the Chinese Permanent Cemetery are clearly marked. Take the second turning on the right.

Ladies lazing: art on the MTR

It's a steep climb, but with the advantage of leaving the pedestrian-unfriendly urban landscape quickly behind. Views of the harbour and of the Lei Yue Mun typhoon shelter open up on your right. After a few rainshelters, a brown Wilson Trail sign finally appears to confirm your route. Turn left to mount the steps, and then left again at the mapboard.

The trail now winds steadily northwards, gaining height to overlook the housing estates and godowns below. The peaks encircling Kowloon can all be seen ahead. At the first fork, turn right. A short rise leads you up to the remains of a battery built shortly after the New Territories were leased to Britain in 1898.

There are emplacements for two giant fixed guns which were able to fire on ships many miles away. These were removed in the 1930s and moved to Stanley, because the government at the time feared an attack from the sea

Yau Tong: at the edge of Kowloon

rather than from land; so when the Japanese invaded from the north in 1941, the battery had no guns. Indian troops held the position for a while before performing a midnight evacuation across the strait to Hong Kong Island.

Morning walkers have planted flowers where the guns once turned, and alcoves which must once have held military supplies are now shrines to popular deities like Kwun Yam and Wong Tai Sin.

You can take an optional detour up to the summit of Devil's Peak, which is topped by the main redoubt. Return to the fork and turn right, then left, following the brown signs. Just before reaching the fort the path mounts the ridgeline, giving you simultaneous views of Victoria Harbour on one side and open seas on the other.

Commanding heights for a gun emplacement

Old and new: Lei Yue Mun and Sai Wan Ho

The fort was completed in 1914, and incorporated the natural rocky outcrops of the peak in its fortifications. It's a commanding position with a 360-degree view. An encircling wall has slits designed for machine guns, and a trench connects the redoubt to the battery below.

Descend the way you came, and return to the road. Turn left now to follow the blue signs to Lei Yue Mun village. After a short while they direct you onto a newly paved stone path on your right, which wends its way across a hillside lush with tall grass. Suddenly, you're again presented with a view of the harbour. Try to time this for dusk or early evening; the skies over the harbour are filled with dozens of kites, circling and swooping on currents of warm air.

The track leads downhill beside a rocky ravine – this coastline was once quarried for stone. Telephone cables and overgrown foundations hint that this hillside was also until recently the site of precarious squatter huts. Soon you reach the village, a motley collection of ramshackle houses with the occasional papaya or banana tree.

Gunners' panorama of Hong Kong Island

All clear: no destroyers on the horizon, only junks and tugboats

Rows of fishing boats at Shau Kei Wan

It's easy to follow the path to the coast. The glittering towers on the opposite shore could not provide a greater contrast to the crumbling houses and jetties on this one. Imagine the scene in 1941, when Royal Artillery, Rajput and Punjabi soldiers made their way down the hill under cover of darkness to be ferried over to Hong Kong Island before the Japanese could arrive. In fact it seems as if this side of the channel has been frozen in time since then, while the other has moved on fully into the 21st century.

Turn left to visit the village's Tin Hau temple, preceded by a pair of cannons and rocks inscribed with Chinese verses. The temple was built in the mid-1700s and was renovated in 1953 after an apparition of Tin Hau reportedly appeared in the clouds.

If you like, you can explore further beyond the temple: the path carries on through its courtyard and past more woebegone residences to an alternately sandy and rocky shoreline with ruined buildings and seawalls from the quarry which operated here. The area is popular with anglers and wargamers. It is in fact Kowloon's last remaining natural coastline. A coastal highway project proposed by the government several years ago was defeated by green groups.

Retracing your steps past the temple, follow the coastline back towards the harbour, through a much busier part of the village. Living rooms are open to the street, with dinner or mahjong games in progress. Shortly you reach an open area beside the harbour, where a beacon sited on boulders is lined up with the end of the old Kai Tak runway. From this point on, you see why Lei Yue Mun is well known among locals: it's one long alley full of seafood vendors and restaurants, a little like Cheung Chau but within easy reach of Kowloon. There's even a connection: the village's school was built by Aw Boon Haw, the philanthropist who funded Cheung Chau's hospital. By all means stop for dinner – there is plenty of choice – but make sure you know in advance how much your selected seafood costs.

Leaving the village, walk around the typhoon shelter to reach the main road. Bus 14C, or any red minibus, will take you back to the MTR at Yau Tong; it's also a short walk to the station, clearly signposted or you could choose to carry on to the pier, where a ferry service runs every half hour to Sai Wan Ho on Hong Kong side. It's a brief but scenic journey on an open-sided ferry – you may even cross the path of a giant cruise liner squeezing through the Lei Yue Mun gap.

Temple defence: cannons and couplets

Sizzling prawns, a Hong Kong favourite

Rocky refuge: Kowloon's last remaining natural shoreline